Agnes Morgan
Fogg Art Museum

Barbizon Revisited

BARBIZON

REVISITED

Essay and catalogue by Robert L. Herbert

Yale University

Clarke & Way, Inc., New York

Letterpress by Clarke & Way. Offset by Meriden Gravure Co. Color by Joh. Enschedé en Zonen

Exhibition Dates

California Palace of the Legion of Honor: September 27–November 4, 1962

Toledo Museum of Art: November 20–December 27, 1962

Cleveland Museum of Art: January 15–February 24, 1963

Museum of Fine Arts, Boston: March 14–April 28, 1963

Under the High Patronage of

SON EXCELLENCE M. HERVÉ ALPHAND, *Ambassadeur de France aux États-Unis*

HIS EXCELLENCY MR. CHARLES E. BOHLEN, *Ambassador of the United States to France*

Sponsored by

The Trustees of the California Palace of the Legion of Honor, San Francisco
MR. WALTER E. BUCK, *President*

The Trustees of the Toledo Museum of Art, MR. HARRY E. COLLIN, *President*

The Trustees of the Cleveland Museum of Art, MR. HAROLD T. CLARK, *President*

The Trustees of the Museum of Fine Arts, Boston, MR. RALPH LOWELL, *President*

Committee of Honor

SON EXCELLENCE M. ANDRÉ MALRAUX, *Ministre d'État, Chargé des Affaires Culturelles*

M. JACQUES JAUJARD, *Membre de l'Institut, Secrétaire Général aux Affaires Culturelles*

M. EDOUARD MOROT-SIR, *Conseiller Culturel près l'Ambassade de France aux États-Unis*

M. GERMAIN BAZIN, *Conservateur en chef du Départment des Peintures, Musée du Louvre*

M. JEAN VERGNET-RUIZ, *Inspecteur Général Honoraire des Musées de Province*

MONSIEUR P. QUONIAM, *Inspecteur Général des Musées de Province*

MM. LES MAIRES *de Amiens, Lille, Montpellier*

M. ROBERT RICHARD, *Musée de Picardie, Amiens*

MR. W. J. H. B. SANDBERG, *Stedelijk Museum, Amsterdam*

DR. GUNTER BUSCH, *Kunsthalle, Bremen*

SR. BENITO QUINQUELA MARTIN, *Museo Nacional de Bellas Artes, Buenos Aires*

MR. KEITH ANDREWS, *The National Gallery of Scotland, Edinburgh*

STUART M. K. HENDERSON, PH. D., *Glasgow Art Gallery and Museum*

DR. ALFRED HENTZEN, *Kunsthalle, Hamburg*

DR. GERT VON DER OSTEN, *Wallraf-Richartz-Museum, Köln*

M. PIERRE MAUROIS, *Palais des Beaux-Arts, Lille*

SIR PHILIP HENDY, *The National Gallery, London*

M. JEAN CLAPARÈDE, *Musée Fabre, Montpellier*

DR. J. C. EBBINGE WUBBEN, *Museum Boymans-van Beuningen, Rotterdam*

MR. W. N. H. VAN DER VORM, *Stichting Willem van der Vorm, Rotterdam*

Acknowledgment

BARBIZON REVISITED is the collaborative undertaking of four museums, the California Palace of the Legion of Honor, San Francisco, the Toledo Museum of Art, the Cleveland Museum of Art and the Museum of Fine Arts, Boston. The privilege of exhibiting these pictures in four cities representing the east coast, the middle west and the west coast, and for an extended period in each, has demanded uncommon generosity on the part of all the lenders. The Trustees and Directors of the collaborating museums are therefore deeply grateful to the museums and private collectors in France, England, Scotland, Germany, the Netherlands and Argentina, as well as in the United States, for their cooperative response to our enterprise and for their sacrifice.

For invaluable assistance in obtaining loans from France we are especially indebted to Messieurs André Malraux, Hervé Alphand, Jacques Jaujard, Jean Vergnet-Ruiz, P. Quoniam, Germain Bazin, Professor André Chastel, Edouard Morot-Sir, Jean Savelli, Pierre Basdevant and Michel Sciama.

In Britain we owe a special debt of gratitude to J. Baer, Esq. of the Hazlitt Gallery, London, who not only assisted in obtaining loans but also graciously undertook on our behalf to assemble for shipment the pictures from England and Scotland.

Robert L. Herbert, Assistant Professor of the History of Art at Yale University, has not only written the critical essay on the Barbizon school and prepared the catalogue, but also has selected the exhibition and assisted in obtaining loans.

For the collaborating museums the Museum of Fine Arts assumed the task of organization and the production of the catalogue. For coordination of information and detail in these undertakings Miss Virginia Fay, Secretary to the Director and Thomas N. Maytham, Assistant in the Painting Department, deserve our special thanks. Others who have earned our gratitude are David B. Little, Secretary and Registrar of the Museum, who has arranged all details of shipment and Carl F. Zahn, Designer for the Museum, for the typography and layout of the catalogue.

P. T. R.

Lenders

A. G. H. Bampfylde, *London*

Mr. and Mrs. S. van Berg, *New York*

Walter P. Chrysler, Jr., *New York*

Col. T. A. H. Coltman, *Grantham, England*

William A. Coolidge, *Topsfield, Massachusetts*

Mme. Jacques Dupont, *Paris*

Jean Ehrmann, *Paris*

John Goelet, *Paris*

César de Hauke, *Paris*

Jerome Hill, *New York*

George Howard, *Yorkshire, England*

Miss Aimée Lamb, *Boston*

Mrs. Henry Potter Russell, *San Francisco*

Sam Salz, *New York*

Mrs. Hannes Schroll, *San Francisco*

Denys Sutton, *London*

John Tillotson, *Bedfordshire, England*

Mrs. Edward L. Tuohy, *Santa Barbara*

Ir. V. W. van Gogh, *Laren, Holland*

Julius H. Weitzner, *New York*

Mrs. John Woolf, *London*

Musée de Picardie, *Amiens*

Stedelijk Museum, *Amsterdam*

Maryland Institute, *Baltimore*

The Walters Art Gallery, *Baltimore*

Museum of Fine Arts, *Boston*

Kunsthalle, *Bremen*

The Brooklyn Museum

Museo Nacional de Bellas Artes, *Buenos Aires*

Albright-Knox Art Gallery, *Buffalo*

Fogg Art Museum, Harvard University, *Cambridge*

The Art Institute of Chicago

The Cincinnati Art Museum

The Cleveland Museum of Art

Denver Art Museum

Tweed Gallery, University of Minnesota, *Duluth*

The Detroit Institute of Arts

The National Gallery of Scotland, *Edinburgh*

Glasgow Art Gallery and Museum

Kunsthalle, *Hamburg*

Wadsworth Atheneum, *Hartford*

Andrew Dickson White Museum of Art, Cornell University, *Ithaca, New York*

Wallraf-Richartz-Museum, *Köln*

Palais des Beaux-Arts, *Lille*

The National Gallery, *London*

The Minneapolis Institute of Arts

Musée Fabre, *Montpellier*

Yale University Art Gallery, *New Haven*

The Solomon R. Guggenheim Museum, *New York*

The Metropolitan Museum of Art, *New York*

Smith College Museum of Art, *Northampton, Massachusetts*

Musée du Louvre, *Paris*

Johnson Collection, *Philadelphia*

Philadelphia Museum of Art

Museum Boymans-van Beuningen, *Rotterdam*

Stichting Willem van der Vorm, *Rotterdam*

City Art Museum of St. Louis

Washington University, *St. Louis*

California Palace of the Legion of Honor, *San Francisco*

Museum of Fine Arts, *Springfield, Massachusetts*

The Toledo Museum of Art

Jewett Arts Center, Wellesley College, *Wellesley, Massachusetts*

Contents

Foreword

THIS IS the first important exhibition of the painters of Barbizon to be undertaken in contemporary times. The last comparable effort took place hardly within the memory of any living person. This was the comprehensive exhibition of the Barbizon school organized by the Barye Monument Society in New York in 1889.

Likewise, this catalogue is only the second serious attempt in the twentieth century to appraise the whole achievement of the school *in extenso*. The last significant work was Prosper Dorbec's essay, *L'Art du Paysage*, which appeared in 1925. To be sure, chapters in numerous modern histories of French art have surveyed the movement, and as late as fifty years ago entire books on the subject from American presses were not uncommon. But these were works of a sentimental, moralistic or popular kind having little factual value or, for us, even readability. While they are interesting as evidence of the long lingering attachment to Barbizon painting and the widespread devotion to its ideals in this country, they are scarcely adequate tools to assist us in our present day quiet but persistent urge to bring into critical focus, to understand and enjoy anew, a school deeply respected and loved by our grandfathers, a school which in a sense lies buried, but refuses to die. It is our hope that this publication will be worthy of a place alongside Moreau-Nélaton's exemplary *catalogues raisonnées* of the individual masters of Barbizon.

That the initiative for this exhibition should be assumed in the United States is not surprising. For while there is no clamor today amongst collectors to acquire Barbizon pictures—even those by Corot, except for his figure pieces—the impact of the school upon our country is evident somewhere on the walls of every older museum. And the storage rooms of the same museums hold an additional harvest of forgotten works, not a few of them masterpieces that have been cleaned and brought forth for this exhibition. The taste for the Barbizon school is part of the history of American culture.

The painters of Barbizon have had only one rival in the hearts of American collectors —the masters of French Impressionism and Post-Impressionism. One would be hard pressed, for example, to state which in number in American collections exceeds the other, the works of Corot and Millet or those of Monet and Renoir. In any case, it is reasonable to say that the understanding and enthusiasm in this country for the earlier masters led to a similar response in the next generation to the masters of Impressionism. In this way, the development of American taste paralleled the dependence of the Impressionist artists themselves upon the achievements of Barbizon. To demonstrate this artistic relationship there has been added to the large group of Barbizon paintings in the exhibition a selection of works by Impressionist painters revealing the influence of the older school on the younger, both immediate and remote.

The paintings of Barbizon were the first contemporary European works to be acquired in significant quantity by Americans. Why, we may ask, was the response to this art so forthcoming and so faithful? The answer lies in the climate of the times and in the cultural background of the American people. Idealistic and rhetorical art inspired by poetry and allegory had never taken a firm hold in America. On the other hand, a faith in nature which amounted to worship was part of the romantic movement of the nine-

46   DUPRÉ.   *Plateau de Belle-Croix.* 1830

teenth century and had already found expression in the success of the new American landscape school. This movement which commenced some twenty years before the importation of the first Barbizon works was part of the general rise of landscape art in the nineteenth century, and in America it settled into a characteristic form of realistic nature poetry related to the ideals of Barbizon. Moreover, in a democratic society the dignity of labor was not only taken for granted, it actually reflected the Puritan ideal, "To work is to pray." It is not surprising then that Millet's laborers—an expression of egalitarian France that shocked the art patrons of Paris—found a natural audience in this country.

One cannot mention the success of the Barbizon school in America without reference to William Morris Hunt. This gifted and idealistic painter from Boston while studying in Paris came into contact with the struggling painters of Barbizon, settled in that village for a time, and became a disciple of Millet. Like Mary Cassatt in relation to the Impressionists thirty years later, it was largely through Hunt's influence, at first in Boston, that Corot and Millet, and then all the Barbizon painters, found their American patrons. From Boston, where Quincy Adams Shaw became Millet's foremost American devotee, the influence spread to all the collecting cities of the country, to New York where William H. Vanderbilt and J. P. Morgan built important collections, to the Potter Palmers in Chicago, to John G. Johnson in Philadelphia, to Emilie Heine in Cincinnati, to Edmund C. Burke in Cleveland, to Arthur J. Secor in Toledo, and to J. J. Hill in St. Paul; to St. Louis, and San Francisco. The collecting of all the painters of the Barbizon school continued unabated for sixty years and for some twenty years overlapped the new enthusiasm for the Impressionists. The result of this activity is an uncounted artistic resource which is only suggested by this exhibition.

While the great majority of works in the exhibition are drawn from American museums and private collections, we have included numerous important works from abroad. In presenting to the best of our ability a balanced and comprehensive survey of the whole movement, certain works in foreign collections were indispensable. Needless to say, there have been disappointments in response to our requests owing to restrictions or to the condition of certain works desired. A very few works could be shown in less than all four museums which have undertaken this exhibition.

It is now over a century since the first American visited Barbizon. That through this exhibition Barbizon be revisited is an opportunity, if not an obligation, overdue.

PERRY T. RATHBONE, *Director*

Museum of Fine Arts, Boston

September, 1962

I also heard the voices of the trees . . .; this whole world of flora lived as deaf-mutes whose signs I divined and whose passions I uncovered; I wanted to talk with them and to be able to tell myself, by this other language—painting—that I had put my finger on the secret of their majesty.

THÉODORE ROUSSEAU

BARBIZON REVISITED

FROM about 1875 to the first World War, British and American tourists making the grand tour visited the village of Barbizon on the northern fringe of Fontainebleau forest, and at nearby Chailly gazed on the sculpted features of Théodore Rousseau and Jean-François Millet, placed together on the same memorial stone. After the Great War, such sentimental feelings were no longer acceptable, and most of the Barbizon artists were relegated to the attic along with other memories of the nineteenth century. We would have been aware that this was an unmerited limbo if we had looked carefully at the art of Barbizon, but prejudice always determines what we choose to see. We rejected Barbizon art because we no longer appreciated the feelings of our grandparents, and therefore of the art they loved but, paradoxically, this meant that we accepted their view that Barbizon painting was indeed sentimental, instead of making up our own minds. Furthermore, the fact that not only English ladies, but also major artists like Cézanne, Van Gogh and Seurat continued to find inspiration in the work of Millet or Rousseau should have taught us that there is a permanence to French art of the mid-century which belies the prevailing view.

French Landscape before 1830

THE HEART of Barbizon art was direct study from nature, be it landscape or the human figure. Barbizon artists were the first to narrow the gap that had traditionally existed between the direct sketch and the finished studio picture. Though Claude Lorrain and Poussin still dominated French landscape at the beginning of the nineteenth century, fresh studies of nature were part of the training of every landscape painter. When Corot's teacher Michallon exhibited in the Salon of 1812 a painting entitled *A Wash-House, study after nature at Aunay*, no eyebrows were raised because the artist did not propose his landscape as anything other than a study. Finished pictures, on the other hand, were invariably studio compositions in which the lessons from such studies were made subordinate to the concept of the "noble landscape." Nature, merely painted as it existed,

---

Note: The text has not been written merely as a commentary upon the paintings and drawings. Instead, the selection of works and the entire catalogue were the result of a whole set of interlocked goals. Given the absence of modern writings on this period, I have provided an extensive text and chronology which stress the least-known aspects: the early years of Barbizon art, and throughout, the work of Rousseau and Millet. Ideally the selection of artists would have included some of the precursors and lesser Barbizon figures, but each such addition would have meant a reduced representation of the main figures. It does include a large number of Salon pictures, the better to recapture the public image of Barbizon art in its own day. For the text I have relied especially on Prosper Dorbec's essay on landscape, and Moreau-Nélaton's magnificent monographs. Citations from the artists can be found in the major studies included in the bibliography.

R. L. H.

lacked two essentials. Firstly, the sense of the creative human mind which should eliminate minor details by a process of artful selection, and rearrange the elements of nature as an idealized whole. The simple reproduction of nature was not creative, but imitative. The resultant landscape could be further embellished with human figures borrowed from the classical tradition since nature alone, even idealized, lacked sufficient interest. Secondly, nature itself had no sense of permanence, which could only result from the same process of idealization. The momentary and the fugitive must be shunned since these are temporal aspects which have no significance in the grand order of nature, and which lure the observer into hedonistic experiences instead of the enduring qualities that rise above the undisciplined present.

The history of Barbizon art is the gradual overthrow of this concept of landscape painting until, with the flowering of Impressionism, its very opposite triumphed: a hedonistic devotion to the present moment. The years between 1830 and 1885, which in landscape should be viewed as an integral period, therefore represent a singular departure from the classicizing Renaissance tradition. And Renaissance it was, for a logical corollary of the noble landscape was its constant references to Italy, to that Italy which was the birthplace of Western civilization, which was the chosen home of Claude and Poussin, and the obligatory starting point for any young painter's career, which provided most landscape painters with their subjects even after their return to France, and which was blessed with that eternal sunshine which ennobled the forms of nature, rather than the moist and fitful North whose constantly changing weather interfered with a rational construction of timeless beauty.

The new view of landscape was essentially anti-classical, and involved the inroads of two Northern schools of art, the Dutch and the British. It cannot be said that these two non-Italian concepts of landscape "caused" Barbizon art for, of course, a painter has to be moving in a certain direction before he will notice the signposts. But even if signposts do not cause a journey, they are essential reference points. An artist cannot suddenly make up his mind to paint what he sees in nature and simply do it, for "what he sees" is not a passive, neutral act, but a complex process in which the artist places between himself and "objective" nature a whole set of conventions, inhibitions and acquired experiences. This screen of sensitivity can change, but when it does, the artist seeks the support of other travellers who have before trodden a similar path. Because the arts of England and the Lowlands are so important for the development of naturalism in France, it is worth summarizing their role before beginning a chronological analysis of Barbizon painting.

English Painting in France

Between 1815 and 1835, French contact with British artists and their work, disrupted by the Revolutionary and Napoleonic era, was renewed with great intensity. Ready access to the British treatment of landscape was provided by many travel books in which visiting artists published views of Paris and its environs, the Channel coast and the region along the Seine. They followed in the footsteps of Thomas Girtin who in 1803 had published twenty aquatints of Paris and its surroundings: Cotman in 1821, Pugin and Gendall also in 1821, Harding and Burnet by 1835, and Turner in 1837, to cite a few outstanding examples. Some of these were published in Paris, and both Harding and Burnet (Burnet's "Notions pratiques sur l'art de la peinture," 1835) gave lessons in British methods. The goal of these topographical landscapes was to record specific sites in France, and such compositions had a new directness and simplicity. Besides travel books, English prints were sold in Paris. The impact of this impressive body of landscape is most visible in the flowering of their French counterparts, various travel books and topographical illustrations which began to mushroom in the mid-thirties and which utilized the talents of Dupré, Jacque and Daubigny. The fact that Jacque went to England in 1836 to learn his trade is strong evidence of the hegemony of the British topographical tradition.

A second way in which French artists learned of British painting was to cross the Channel themselves. Whereas only Corot and Daubigny went to Italy, the traditional mecca of young French artists, several of the Barbizon painters visited England: Dupré in 1834, Jacque in 1836–38, Troyon in 1853, Corot in 1862, and Daubigny in 1866 and again in 1870–71 (when Monet and Pissarro were also in London). They had been preceded by Géricault in 1820–22, Guillon Lethière (Rousseau's teacher) in 1821, and Delacroix in 1825. At the same time, the many paintings of themes from Byron and Shakespeare by Delacroix, Vernet, Scheffer and others denoted a veritable Anglomania.

Equally important was the presence in Paris of British artists and their paintings. In addition to those artists whose travel books have already been mentioned, most important British landscape artists (Constable the notable exception) worked for a time in France. Turner made frequent visits and David Cox also, in 1829 and 1832; William Wyld seems to have lived steadily in Paris in the twenties and was already in Algiers when Delacroix arrived there in 1832; John Harding worked in Paris for some time, and Constable's friend, the engraver Reynolds, had a studio there in the late twenties. The British exhibited regularly in the Paris Salon. Their apogee came with the famous Salon of 1824, when some thirty British paintings were shown, and they received a number of prizes, from Glover's in 1814 to Harding's in 1834.

Of the British artists active in France, Bonington and the Fielding brothers are the most important. Delacroix met Bonington about 1816, and their intimacy had the most profound effects on the chief painter of the French Romantic school. Huet also knew Bonington, and other artists could see his work by visiting dealer's shops or the Salons (Baron Gros in 1819 urged his students to study Bonington's watercolors). The several Fielding brothers were friends of both Delacroix and Huet; Delacroix shared a studio with Thales Fielding in 1823 and was his guest in London two years later. Stendhal recorded their collaboration on their Salon paintings of 1824, each having helped the other. Newton Fielding's lithographs published in Paris in 1828 and 1829 inspired Decamps' early animal pictures, and three of the four brothers, together with Bonington, helped illustrate Baron Taylor's "Voyages Pittoresques."

Constable, though he never came to France, had the most decided influence on French landscape. Géricault was not the only French artist who became enthusiastic over Constable even before the Salon of 1824. A certain Regnier, a French landscape painter, owned a Constable which Delacroix raved about when he saw it in November, 1823. The dealer Arrowsmith, who had met the British painter in 1822, brought from England three of Constable's works for the Salon of 1824, where they were so popular that they were moved to the principal exhibition room shortly after the opening. Constable was awarded a gold medal. Thereafter his paintings became more and more familiar to the French. He sent his *White Horse* to an exhibition in Lille in 1825, and just a year later Amadée Pichot, in his "Lettres sur l'Angleterre," proclaimed the superiority of Constable and the English school over French landscape. Major artists like Paul Huet and Camille Flers were by then painting in a pronouncedly Constablesque manner, and Huet freely circulated his oil copies after the British master. Arrowsmith the dealer, who was also a painter, was accused by a critic in 1827 of pastiching Constable, a logical result of his collection of Constables which were numerous enough to embellish a "Constable Room" in his shop by the early thirties. Among other dealers, Susse and Mme. Hulin both had Constables and Boningtons at the same period. These modest facts take on new significance when we learn that Rousseau was a friend of Arrowsmith and that he, Dupré and other Barbizon artists sold and exhibited paintings with Susse and Mme. Hulin. No wonder then that Thoré-Bürger, Rousseau's life-long friend, wrote in 1863 ("Histoire des peintres, Ecole anglaise") that Constable was a major force in the regeneration of French landscape by the School of 1830.

Lowlands Painting in France

When Delacroix met Bonington, the young British artist was copying Lowlands paintings, an act which symbolizes the link between the two Northern schools. The precedent of Dutch art was an important factor in the awakening of English landscape at the turn of the century. Like the Barbizon artists later, the British, although retaining an admiration for Claude, Poussin and the classical tradition, turned to Dutch landscape of the seventeenth century to redefine their attitude toward nature. Therefore the incursion of British landscape in France after 1815 helped open the French painters' eyes to the attractions of Lowlands art. Here the best evidence lies in the paintings themselves, and so overwhelming is it that no documentation is necessary. Rousseau, Troyon, Daubigny and Jacque all made copies of Dutch animal and landscape paintings; Rousseau and Millet jointly bought a van Goyen which they divided by the wisdom of Solomon, cutting it in two; Rousseau owned four paintings attributed to Bruegel, and about fifty prints by Ruysdael, Rembrandt, A. van de Velde, van Goyen, A. van Ostade, van der Neer and others; Millet had an even more impressive collection of Lowlands art: five paintings attributed to Bruegel, one van Hemessen, and literally hundreds of prints, including Rembrandt and van Ostade. Thoré-Bürger, their close friend, chose Holland for his place of exile after the 1848 Revolution, and in 1858 began to publish his major works on the art of the Netherlands. The crisis of Troyon's life was his year in the Lowlands in 1847; Corot in 1854 and Daubigny in 1871 confirmed their interest in Dutch art by brief visits there; Jongkind and Boudin, fraternal allies of the Barbizon artists, helped assimilate Dutch art and pass it on to the Impressionists (Jongkind by birthright, since he was Dutch).

To be sure, Chardin and Greuze are proof enough that Lowlands art had not been ignored in the eighteenth century (even Boucher was inspired by van Ostade and Teniers in his rustic scenes), but French landscape remained immune to the Northern concept of nature until the next century. By the early thirties, critics had noticed the presence of Ruysdael and Hobbema in the work of Dupré and Rousseau, and thereafter parallels with Lowlands art were the common coin of art criticism. It surged through French art in three allied types of painting, animal painting, genre and landscape. By 1851 a number of specialists in animal painting began to win notice, and soon there was an entire French school modelled upon Cuyp and Potter: Brascassat, Flers, the Leleux brothers (friends of Daubigny), Philippe Rousseau (no relation to Théodore), Veyrassat, Decamps (a friend of most of the Barbizon artists), Rosa Bonheur, Jacque, Troyon and Diaz. Courbet too can be invoked, since his animals often derive from Frans Snyders (he visited the Lowlands in 1847). French genre painting of the period, echoing a knowledge of Bruegel, de Hooch, Maes, Teniers, the van Ostades, Steen and Rembrandt (Vermeer was only revived after 1858—by Thoré-Bürger!), involved most of the animal painters, but also genre specialists like Meissonier and Bonvin, both known to the Barbizon artists, and above all, Millet. Landscape painting is the third of the categories in which Dutch art was a leaven. Every major landscapist active in France after 1850 absorbed the pulsations emanating from the northeast. Ruysdael, Hobbema, Rembrandt, van de Velde, van Goyen, Wouvermans, van der Neer, Koninck and Seghers were all important and so clear is their contribution that one can distinguish their separate styles refracted in the pool of French art.

Plein-Air Painting before 1830

Although fresh paintings of nature were considered only the necessary groundwork for finished paintings, it is obvious that after 1800 artists like Valenciennes and Michallon lavished great affection on outdoor paintings and thought them worthy of exhibition, albeit carefully labeled as "studies." By the early twenties, plein-air painting was so popular that there were regular summer colonies of artists established in Fontainebleau forest, along the Channel coast, and in the region of Sèvres and Saint-Cloud. Fontainebleau was the most favored because it had the virtue of being near Paris while still offering wild and untouched areas, unlike the forests of Compiègne and Saint-Cloud which were more like parklands. As the decade of the twenties unfolded, three villages on the fringe of the forest drew more and more artists: Marlotte, Chailly and Barbizon. There are two main reasons why painting out-of-doors seems to have increased so rapidly. First, the enormous growth in the number of painters of all categories and, therefore, of landscapists. Second, the gradual shift in subject matter from historical and figure painting to landscape. The fact that the official prix de Rome for landscape was established in 1817 is a clue to the development of nature worship in France.

The first major landscape artist to appear in the twenties was Paul Huet (1803–69), who occupies a peculiar position in the evolution of Barbizon art, since he is more important for the example he set than for his painting itself. A friend of Delacroix and

Bonington, he shared the new enthusiasm for British art, copied Constable's paintings, and was considered by the burgeoning Romantics as their one landscape artist. From 1819, when still a boy, he did a number of handsome watercolors of the Sèvres region which display a knowledge of British techniques blended with a native penchant for simple statement. Huet met Delacroix in 1822 when he was already an accomplished painter of nature, having absorbed both British and Dutch traditions. He travelled widely in France after 1824 and brought back to the Romantic circles in Paris landscapes which proved that French sites interpreted by a French painter could at last rival the established schools outside the country, and the classicizing tradition of French landscape which the Romantics associated with the artistic enemy.

Corot, seven years Huet's senior, began painting seriously out-of-doors about 1822, and before he left for Italy three years later, he had worked all along the Channel coast, in Paris and its environs, and in Fontainebleau. During his first long stay in Italy, his plein-air paintings are rather close to those of Valenciennes or Michallon, but blessed with a limpid beauty that no other artist could approach. In 1829, after his return from Italy, he went on a long campaign in Normandy, Brittany and Fontainebleau. The few paintings that can be identified from that year show no interest, however, in the current Anglo-Dutch fashion, partly because his apprenticeship in Italy fortified the Mediterranean part of his heritage.

Rousseau, sixteen years younger than Corot, began to paint at an early age. His first plein-air work is from 1827, when he was only fifteen. From 1827 to 1829 he painted occasionally at Fontainebleau and adjacent Moret (No. 82), in a manner fully as original as Corot's, perhaps a bit more vigorous.

1830-1839

THE REVOLUTION of July, 1830, engendered an enthusiasm in Paris which we can recapture today only with difficulty, an excitement which lasted for nearly a decade until it gave way to the disillusionment that ultimately brought about the more drastic Revolution of 1848. The young Romantics, nearly all ardent radicals, greeted the July Monarchy as a symbol of their personal victory, for they were the intellectuals of the Orleanist party. Nearly all the young Barbizon artists found their first patrons among the Orleanist faction, including the Duc d'Orléans himself and Paul Casimir-Périer. It was the decade of Hugo's triumph; of the founding of the Petit Cénacle by Gautier, Borel and Gérard de Nerval; of Delacroix' incontestable claim to a high place, if not to academic honors; of the appearance of Stendhal's two most important novels; of Michelet, Sainte-Beuve, Barbier, Alexandre Dumas, Musset, Vigny, Lamartine, Meyerbeer and Balzac.

With the presentation of Hugo's "Hernani" in February, 1830, the young literati claimed their first major success. The painters' laurels were won in the Salon of 1831. For many years yet they had to withstand the opposition of the entrenched academic forces, but the Romantic school captured the leading critics with a solid phalanx headed

ROUSSEAU. *The Bridge at Moret.* 1828–29

by Delacroix, Decamps, Devéria, Léopold Robert, Delaroche, Ary Scheffer and Horace Vernet. An unusually large number of landscapes were exhibited, including those of Corot, Diaz, Dupré, Rousseau and Huet. Huet was pre-eminent with nine paintings and four watercolors. He appended verses from Hugo to his *Sun setting behind an old abbey situated in the middle of the woods*, leaving no doubts that he was a full-fledged Romantic. His essential characteristics, established in 1831, were to continue virtually unchanged for the rest of his life: moody landscapes of primeval forest or yawning chasm. He also exhibited views of Rouen, Avignon and other French sites, but instead of finding a radical naturalism when we look back on these works, we see a blending of Anglo-Dutch tendencies with a substructure of classical composition derived from Claude, Poussin and Salvator Rosa. Huet remained a Romantic, while the Barbizon artists gradually moved toward a frank naturalism.

Rousseau

Huet dominated landscape in 1831, but his place was usurped in 1833 by a young man around whom centered the development of French landscape for the subsequent fifteen years: Théodore Rousseau. Only eighteen years old, Rousseau had returned to Paris in the fall of 1830 from a long stay in the Auvergne mountains. His talents were recognized by Ary Scheffer, who exhibited the Auvergne landscapes in his studio for the enlightenment of his visitors. These extraordinary compositions of rushing mountain torrents, rocky escarpments and wild valleys were painted with an energetic brushwork and heightened color that make us think today of the expressionist styles of the early twentieth century. For Rousseau's contemporaries, they were the confirmation of Romanticism and embodied the sublime energy and the tragic solitude of Byron, Shakespeare, Dante and Goethe. Rousseau soon joined the young intellectual radicals in Paris, the circle which looked to Hugo and Delacroix as their heroes. By 1833 he was associated with a group who tried, unsuccessfully, to fight the offical Salon: Borel, Préault, Daumier, Jeanron, and others. But he was less preoccupied with politics than they, and with Scheffer as his protector, he was accepted by the Orleanists. Between 1833 and 1840, his paintings were bought by the Duc d'Orléans, the Prince de Joinville, Paul Casimir-Périer and the Duc de Broglie (who commissioned a painting to be given to Guizot). Artists his own age began to gather around him: Jacque (1833), Dupré (1834) and Diaz (1837). The critic Thoré (later Thoré-Bürger) became his intimate friend and defender in 1833. When his *Descent of the Cattle* was rejected by the Salon in 1836, and his *Avenue of Chestnut Trees* two years later, Scheffer rallied Delacroix and George Sand to his defense. By the end of the decade, Rousseau's reputation was established as the most important landscape painter of the new generation.

His first Salon picture, a studio painting of the Auvergne exhibited in 1831, was submerged under the attention Huet received, but his *View taken along the Norman Coast at Granville* in the 1833 Salon, following upon his lionization by Scheffer's circle, brought him instant fame. This large painting, bought at the time by Scheffer but in Leningrad since Rousseau's death, is a remarkable document for the history of French landscape.

Despite its undoubted originality, it breathes the air of Constable and the Dutch. It is no exaggeration to view it as a French counterpart to the British painter's *Haywain* which had so stirred Paris in 1824. The broad sweep of the foreground includes a pond and a horse-drawn wagon; the middleground has houses largely hidden by copses of trees; the sea only appears as a thin band at the horizon. A prominent rocky outcropping and a decayed tree-trunk along the left edge give the composition a moody intensity that recalls Ruysdael, as does also the tight brushwork.

The *Descent of the Cattle* (No. 88), rejected by the Salon of 1836, was a *cause célèbre* and marks the height of Rousseau's most overtly Romantic phase. Cattle are descending the Alps for their winter pasturage in the valleys below; they pass down a writhing, rocky slope between enormous pines, the whole heaved up on the surface of the canvas with only a bit of turbulent sky showing at the top. Now rather ruined by a free use of bitumen, the painting had a liquid freedom unacceptable to the classical landscape artists, let alone its overtones of Byron and Dante, as though the cattle were descending into the murky bowels of the earth. A third example of Rousseau's major paintings of the thirties, the *Valley of Tiffauge* (No. 91), shows another facet of his Romantic temperament. A detailed rendering of rocks, water and marshy growth occupies the foreground, an astonishing variety of textures. It was a side of nature that had never before been considered worthy of a finished picture, and it was as a result given the derisive nicknames *The Muddle* and *The Soup of Weeds*. For more enlightened spirits it showed—to adapt a later phrase of Millet—that the trivial could be made to serve the sublime. Where in the *Descent of the Cattle* he had been attracted by a splendid spectacle of the Alps in autumn, in this painting he gave a visual statement of his passionate closeness to the innocuous details of nature, a quasi-scientific concern that foretells the great fascination for natural sciences that so characterizes the entire mid-century in Europe and America.

He had meanwhile spent most of his summers painting from nature, in Normandy and Brittany, in the Alps for one season, in the Vendée and yet more often at Barbizon. Most of his studies are free and relatively calm in mood. *The Jetty at Granville* (No. 86) has a robust texture that is made the more surprising by its unusual horizontal format. In contrast to its opaque tones, the *Plain of Chailly* (No. 87) of about two years later has a delicate transparency that makes us aware of how important British watercolors were for the Barbizon artists. By its very nature, watercolor produces translucent tones which provide a facsimile of nature's harmonizing light, and in his search for such a unity, Rousseau often achieved a similar effect in diluted oils.

Corot

Like Rousseau, Corot maintained a distinction between his large paintings for exhibition, and his more numerous studies from nature. The public rightly concluded that he was an artist in the established classical tradition, for in addition to nine paintings of Italian sites, he sent to the Salons of the thirties *Hagar, Diana surprised at her Bath, Saint Jerome,* and *Silenus.* The fact that he exhibited paintings of Fontainebleau in 1831, 1833

and 1834 surprised no one, for his comrades d'Aligny and Bertin also submitted Fontainebleau subjects those years, and they were more thoroughly rooted in the Italianate
school.

But there were undercurrents in his art that brought Corot and Rousseau closer than
would seem likely at first glance. For one thing, they both were fond of the same sites:
Normandy, Brittany, Fontainebleau, the Auvergne, and the environs of Paris, although
Corot ranged more widely than his younger compatriot. For another, Corot also felt the
effects of Dutch painting. The first signs of an interest in Lowlands art are found in his
paintings of Paris in 1830. By 1831 it became a strong current, and until 1834 he went
through a virtual Dutch phase. *Farm at Recouvrières* (No. 3) and *Cottages and Mills*
(John Hay Whitney) of 1831 are the nineteenth-century heirs of van de Velde's *The
Artist and his Family* (Rijksmuseum, Amsterdam). His views of Soissons of 1833 remind
us of Ruysdael's famous *Haarlem from the dunes of Overveen* (Berlin). Ruysdael was
for Corot, as well as for Dupré and Rousseau, the most important Dutch master in the
thirties. His Salon picture of 1833, *A Ford in the Forest of Fontainebleau* (collection unknown) is identical in all major elements to the archetypal Ruysdael composition of a
road in the country. We can measure the importance of the Northern concept of landscape in the thirties when we remember that this painting was accompanied by Rousseau's *View of Granville* in the same Salon, both owing a debt to the Dutch and both
sharing common devices, such as the horse-drawn wagon to one side of each composition.
Corot's Italian orientation and his temperament make the Dutch component less obvious than in Rousseau's case. He straightened out the tree trunks, used flatter and more
uniform textures, and gave to the architecture of nature a special crispness. However,
he was at times intrigued by the emotional, writhing terrains we link with Rousseau.
His *Fontainebleau, Artist Walking over a Rocky Terrain* (private collection) of 1828–30
and the *Quarry of La Chaise-à-Marie at Fontainebleau* (Ghent) of 1830–33, for example,
are compositions in which plastic and heaving rocks occupy more than half the surface.

Dupré

Dupré had a role in the thirties second only to Rousseau (Corot caused little stir that
decade). He was only a year older than Rousseau, and also began painting and drawing
at a tender age. He exhibited regularly in the Salon from 1831 to 1839 and took part in
the exciting artists' world of Paris where, because he was more articulate than his com-
panion, he became the painter-spokesman for the new landscape. He received his first
wide notice in the press in 1833, when he won a second-class medal. Perhaps through
Rousseau whom he met the following year, he joined the circle of radicals which included
Thoré, Borel, Daumier, and Préault, and he began contributing lithographs to the
journal "L'Artiste" in 1835. His seven paintings in the Salon of 1839 guaranteed him a
major place in French landscape art.

From his earliest dated works of 1827 until 1832, Dupré's style was dominated by
Claude Lorrain and the eighteenth-century French tradition he had absorbed as a porcelain painter, but with an admixture of Anglo-Dutch (not yet very strong) and a native

frankness that is visible in his *Plateau de Belle-Croix* (No. 46). His subjects were views of the forests of Montmorency, Fontainebleau, the Limousin and the Haute-Vienne, most of which he treated as open parks, with a visible restraint and careful organization. Several were labeled "studies after nature," but they have a feeling of studio compositions since he looked at nature with preconceived notions of organization more accentuated than in Rousseau's or Corot's case. In the Salon of 1833 his *Supper*, again subtitled "sketch from life," had a marked dose of Lowlands genre painting, an evolution confirmed the next year in his *Interior of a Cottage in Berry* (formerly collection Faure), clearly inspired by Teniers and van Ostade. A trip to England in 1834 introduced him directly to British art, and during the rest of the decade he slowly integrated his early Claudesque style with the Anglo-Dutch. Already by 1836 he had developed the one composition which became his favorite: half of the foreground represents a pond or marsh; the other half has a band of water along the bottom; in the middle distance is a prominent copse of trees; on the opposite side, further back, is a projection of land with a cottage or a small group of trees; the whole is surmounted by a lively sky. The essentials of this archetypal composition were derived from Holland, but the careful separation of the different elements and the tendency to silhouette masses of foliage against the sky, stem from Claude. It seems likely that this and two or three other defined organizational schemes preceded those of Rousseau, who admitted that Dupré taught him how to construct a composition.

Diaz

Diaz apparently did not take part in the informal circle of artists and writers around Thoré and Rousseau but, paradoxically, he was the painter closest to Gautier's and Borel's "Petit Cénacle." They created a fad for Rococo art which Diaz espoused in his *scènes galantes,* in which he combined the style of the eighteenth century with that, equally faddish, of Correggio, Prud'hon, Bonington and Delacroix. His groups of young women were frequently given Turkish surroundings, making him an ally of Decamps, Marilhat and other painters in Delacroix' orbit. Aside from a battle scene and a view of a Scots castle (reflecting the English craze), both in the Salon of 1835, he mainly exhibited bathers, nymphs and galantes. The profound impression Rousseau made on him when they met in 1837 was evident in his three landscapes, one of them a Fontainebleau subject, in the Salon of that year.

Troyon

Troyon was less wilfully decorative than Diaz, although they both began as porcelain painters, a trade which Troyon followed throughout the thirties. His Salon pictures of 1833 and 1835 were views of Sèvres and Saint-Cloud, near the state porcelain works. From 1836 to 1839 he travelled more widely, especially in Brittany and the environs of Argenton. The few paintings that can be identified from this period have a light and crisp palette, bright greens and yellows predominant, traceable to his working with porcelain glazes. Combined with a dispassionate temperament and an affiliation with the decorative landscapes of the eighteenth century, the result was an almost arcadian simplicity in contrast to the heavy colors and textures of Rousseau and Dupré. An occasional painting pronouncedly Claudesque in manner points to the ultimate source of his composition. The only hints of Lowlands art are indirect, coming from a respect for Rousseau which appears in the late thirties.

Jacque, Daubigny and Millet

The other Barbizon artists were later in starting. Jacque devoted the decade to learning his trade as a printmaker. Daubigny too began his career as an illustrator, after a trip to Italy in 1836. Millet arrived in Paris from Cherbourg in 1837 and began more sophisticated professional studies.

1840–1847

THE YEARS 1840 to 1847 began in a conservative mood, reflecting the general disenchantment with the July Monarchy, and ended with the Revolution of 1848, when that disillusionment acquired explosive force. In 1840 and 1841 there was a sudden rise in the number of religious paintings (Daubigny, Troyon and Corot included), in 1848 an equally abrupt appearance of socially-conscious pictures. The artistic world was divided into several distinct channels. Ingres' influence spread further and his chief disciple, Flandrin, made his appearance. Delacroix, though far from being accepted by the Academy, exhibited regularly, and the Romantics could acclaim the successes of Scheffer, Devéria and Vernet as well. With Delacroix and Vernet, Decamps and Marilhat established an orientalizing trend (in which Diaz participated). Spanish art, following the opening of the Spanish Gallery in 1838 and the Musée Standish in 1842, became a new fad that seduced many artists, among them the young Millet and Courbet. Animal and genre painting increased in importance, with Rosa Bonheur and Meissonier, both owing an immense debt to Lowlands painting, appearing alongside Brascassat and the Leleux brothers. Aside from landscape, only this latter current entered prominently into the new naturalism which triumphed in 1848.

Rousseau

Rousseau was excluded from the Salon in the forties, but he continued to be the focus of the developments in landscape. His art was known to a wide circle of progressive critics and artists, his patrons were more numerous (Collot, Baroilhet, Didier, Dugléré), and he managed to exhibit outside the Salon, in his own studio and in Dupré's, with the dealers Durand-Ruel, Deforges, Susse and Léopold, in exhibitions organized by Baron Taylor on the boulevard Bonne-Nouvelle, and in the foyer of the Odéon theater. The illustrations of Salon paintings published annually in the journals like "L'Artiste" register his progressive influence on other artists. He managed to sell enough paintings to live modestly and he continued his travels, with major campaigns in the Berry and the Bordeaux regions in addition to his regular seasons in the environs of Paris. Nonetheless, exclusion from the Salon meant that he had fewer occasions to finish major paintings, and this perverse freedom resulted in his giving an even larger amount of his time to studies from nature. He completed relatively few large pictures from 1840 to 1847, although he began a number which he terminated later.

The long season of 1842 in the Berry was one of the great artistic crises of Rousseau's life. There he plunged into several months of agonized solitude during which he developed new types of compositions and new attitudes toward nature which were to determine the whole future course of his art. Only thirty years old, the young artist looked back on a decade of notoriety that revolved around his introspective paintings of somber intensity, whereas he now felt equally strongly the need for a more calm and objective view of nature. His letters from Berry to his friends are full of self-torture. To Dupré he wrote that he lived in "the frightening silence of a desert." "What evil spirit," he said, "pushed me into creating around myself a solitude which has been so bitter! . . . Ah! my dear Dupré, with our wretched passion for art we are dedicated to a perpetual torment, unceasingly we think that we have touched upon a truth which after all escapes us."

Perhaps the shock of being in a region dominated by flat plains, in contrast to his habitual preference for wooded interiors, required of him new efforts to incorporate his passions in art and would alone have forced him into a new pattern of thinking. Moreover, the moist plains of the Berry produced an oppressively humid and changing atmosphere (*Marais de la Souterraine*, No. 92) which suited his melancholy mood but proved difficult to render in painting. Unaided by the writhing trees of Fontainebleau or the grandiose mountains of the Jura, whose forms so readily incarnate human passions, and bent upon disciplining his emotions, Rousseau developed three types of composition. *Under the Birches* (No. 95) is one of these, characterized by a flat strip in the foreground which is dominated by a screen or copse of trees in the middle distance; the low horizon line brings the sky down into the bottom half of the composition, with the result that the whole is marked by horizontal planes parallel to the surface. A second type speaks for itself, simply a broad, deep plain dotted with trees or marshy ponds. The third, represented by *Village in Berry* (No. 93), is very familiar from Dutch painting, especially Hobbema: a level strip of land in the foreground, traversed by a path, brook or pond moving diagonally into the middle distance toward a group of buildings nestled among trees; this main mass is usually to one side, with an opening on the other leading to the distance, but sometimes it is centrally located with a screen of trees placed slightly in front and to one side.

Rousseau returned to flat country in 1844, after a year in the Paris region, and the choice of the Landes near Bordeaux confirms the evolution of the Berry campaign. *Four Communal (Communal Baking-Oven)* is of the first type of composition, with a central copse of trees parallel to the picture plane; *A Marsh in the Landes*, the famous painting in the Louvre completed in 1852, is of the second, and *Farm in the Landes* of the third type (the *Four* and the *Farm* were worked on throughout Rousseau's life for his patron Hartmann). In these paintings of 1842 to 1844, Rousseau's intense mood is at first glance suppressed, but despite the calm order that prevails, close observation reveals an almost obsessive attention to detail, with a concomitant tight brushstroke, and above all, a new luminosity. The moist air of autumn, of a mixed grey-blue density, permeates the compositions and gives a sense of tense expectancy. A delicate balance of light and weather is made explicit in Rousseau's subtitles, *Effect of late afternoon, autumn in the Landes* or *Effect of noontime, stormy sky*. His devotion to the effects of weather puts him squarely in the tradition which leads from Constable to Monet. He liked to discuss what he and Dupré called the "great secret" of nature, luminosity, and the means of creating the effects of natural light with the artificial techniques of painting. The better to observe nature, he developed several aids which foretell those of the Impressionists. He constructed an unusual easel on which he could stretch paper for his drawings out-of-doors (he apparently always began by drawing, usually on tinted paper), invented new ways of priming both paper and canvas, and built lean-tos resembling hunters' blinds which sheltered him from the weather and gave him a privacy as he eavesdropped on nature.

The same concern for particular aspects of weather was the origin of one of his most controversial paintings, *Le Givre* (No. 96). In the winter of 1844–45, with a burst of furious energy, he set about capturing the effects of frost on the slopes of Valmondois. Frost, that is, not the particular site, was the subject. He chose a lurid sunset to surmount the frosty terrain partly because it reflected his intense mood, and partly because the dark tones and ruddy hues set off the light tones and the greens of the foreground.

The gloomy sunset of *Le Givre* reminds us that Rousseau's new devotion to the luminosity of nature and open plains was only one side of his art. He continued to paint highly Romantic compositions like the *Forest in Winter* (formerly Widener collection), begun in December, 1846, a view of the Bas-Bréau in Fontainebleau which pulls out all the stops of the artist's organ: gaunt and twisted trees, troubled sunset, stormy sky. When it was exhibited in 1847, Thoré likened it to Rembrandt, Shakespeare and Hobbema.

Corot

For Corot the years 1840–47 marked the general recognition of his talent and the development of several subjects and compositions which he followed for the rest of his life. Largely ignored in the thirties, he won more important patrons and state commissions in the next decade. Official recognition came with his Legion of Honor in 1846, and by that time Baudelaire and others had become his champions in the press. He continued to roam unceasingly, with his third trip to Italy in 1843, and important seasons in the Morvan (east-central France), Normandy, Brittany, and the environs of Paris. He still did not exhibit his studies from nature in the Salon, but instead subjects from the grand tradition: a monk reading and a flight into Egypt (1840), Democritus (1841), Sodom (1844), Homer, and Daphnis and Chloë (1845), as well as large studio landscapes. Over this span of years he evolved the misty, Claudesque style of composite landscapes which were his chief claim to public attention. His decorations for the home of his friend Robert at Nantes (Louvre) in 1840–42, and his *Environs of Naples* (Springfield) of the 1841 Salon expose the origins of this aspect of his style: Claude Lorrain and the eighteenth-century. Other paintings, like *Homer and the Shepherds* (Saint-Lô) of 1845, are more closely related to the other half of the classical heritage, whose patron saint was Poussin.

Infinitely more modern to our eyes are his unpretentious paintings of smaller scale, usually done from nature. Their careful drawing and crisp harmonies, each plane usually of a uniform and matte texture, indicate that we tend to exaggerate the number and importance of paintings actually done out-of-doors, but they were certainly painted with constant reference to the sites. Luminosity is attained not by means of Rousseau's pervasive and constantly modulated atmosphere, but by the broad harmonies of planes of light hue and value. Contrast, for example, the *Church at Lormes* (No. 7) with Rousseau's *Village in Berry*, probably only a year apart in date. Corot's paint is opaque and uniformly mixed with white, whatever the hue, resulting in an accord of textures that unifies the whole; the greater flatness of the different planes please us, children of the twentieth century, more than the transparent tones of Rousseau.

Once again, however, we should not overlook the bonds between the two artists. They both pushed landscape art in the same direction, toward a new naturalism and a new clarity of light. And Corot's Romanticism is just as much in evidence as Rousseau's, but given their opposed temperaments, it is expressed in his nostalgic souvenirs of Italy and the classical past, rather than in the desolate solitudes and doleful sunsets of France in which Rousseau steeped himself.

Dupré

Dupré's work of the forties has fallen into an oblivion from which it proves difficult to extricate. He did not appear in the Salon after 1839 and the few works he exhibited on the boulevards and in dealers' shops (the same exhibitions in which Rousseau took part) give us only a glimpse of his activity. From 1840 to 1847 he travelled less, spending much of his time at l'Isle-Adam and Paris, often sharing quarters with Rousseau. His major campaigns outside the capital were in the Landes, with Troyon in 1843 and with Rousseau the next year. We know more of his ideas than of his painting, for he continued to be an articulate spokesman for the new school. He shared Rousseau's concern with the luminosity of nature (it was on Dupré's urging that Rousseau went to the Berry and the Landes). "The sky is behind the tree, in the tree, in front of the tree," he said, and critics pointed out these extraordinary skies which he brought forward to the surface with thick pigments and heavy brushwork. A persistent melancholy was also noticed. Unlike the other Barbizon artists who worked simultaneously in the two main currents of the period, the naturalistic and the more Romantic, Dupré seems to have left behind painting directly from nature as the decade progressed. His thick pigments, rather dark palette (enlivened, however, with colors habitually referred to by the critics as "jewel-like"), and Dutch-inspired compositions produced viscous harmonies which came more from an *a priori* concept of painting than from fresh examinations of nature. "Nature is nothing, man is everything." "Nature is only the pretext. Art is the goal, passing through the individual." Such were the aphorisms by which Dupré specified his attitudes. He also said that he was fond of accidents which took place on his palette, sometimes superior to

95   ROUSSEAU.   *Under the Birches* (Le Curé). 1842–44

7   COROT.   *The Church at Lormes.* c. 1841

nature's own colors. Within the matrix of his Rembrandtesque chiaroscuro, we occasionally find such happy accidents. It is fortunate that *The Duck Pond* (No. 48) survives from the period of 1845–48, because it proves that alongside his move toward the rather stereotyped compositions which henceforth dominated his work, Dupré could still create more personal harmonies. It is close to Rousseau in its tight brushwork, but its sky is Dupré's own interpretation of nature's "great secret."

Daubigny

Bad luck has it also that few of Daubigny's paintings before 1848 can be located, but fortunately he made etchings of his Salon paintings, and we have all his independent etchings, woodcuts, lithographs and illustrations. His livelihood came from his graphic work and, although it is not certain, it is likely that what painting he had time for was destined entirely for the Salon. His compositions reveal a potpourri of styles typical of a young painter of the period. *Saint Jerome* in the Salon of 1840, based on a trip to the Alps, was an attempt to rival Huet's version of the noble landscape. *Choisy-le-Roi* and *Le Carrefour du Nid de l'Aigle* of 1843 and 1844 show the continued assimilation of Ruysdael and Hobbema that was already in evidence by 1838, but the fan-shaped foliage and some of the spatial devices register an amalgamation of the Claudesque tradition as well. *Le Ru de Valmondois*, painted in 1846 and exhibited the following year, is reminiscent of Corot's large studio landscapes and *The Valley of the River Cousin* (Louvre) of 1847 is his last venture in the noble landscape, its broad and simple lines stemming from the classical tradition.

His future is discovered more readily in his graphic work, in which these several currents are found, but compounded by a greater naturalism. His many prints for travel books, magazines, song sheets and the like come from the topographical tradition of landscape popularized by the British a generation earlier. Some of them are vignettes and decorated pages which have an eighteenth-century flavor parallel to the contemporary work of Diaz and Millet. In 1845 his etchings are still Romantic in feeling (moonrises, storms) and Rembrandt lies behind his style, but it is a Romantic-Naturalism whose directness and simplicity become increasingly important. The etching *Sheep-fold* of 1846 identifies the year when the new naturalism becomes predominant, although his *Bathers* of the same year, subtitled *Souvenir of the Ru de Valmondois*, is straight out of Corot's Salon landscapes.

Troyon

By the late thirties Troyon had become a professional landscape artist, and no longer worked as a porcelain painter. Instead of views of Sèvres and Saint-Cloud, his subjects of the forties are of Brittany, Orléans and Fontainebleau. Most of them were labelled "studies," but each Salon had a major landscape and he won official notice with second and first-class medals in 1840 and 1846. *Tobias and the Angel* (No. 102) of 1841 was his only essay in the grand tradition. *Road in the Woods* (No. 103) seems to be more typical of his work of this period. It has the lightness of an artist trained in porcelain decoration, but with a solidity that may have resulted from his increased contact with his fellow landscapists (he became friends with Rousseau and Dupré in 1843, and began that year to frequent Fontainebleau). The year of 1847 spent in the Lowlands changed him over-night into an animal painter, presumably because he had already absorbed in Paris the fashion for Dutch painting. Animal painting, fortified by his training as a landscapist, was thereafter the substance of his prominence.

Diaz

From 1840 to 1847 Diaz exhibited only four landscapes, the rest of his many Salon sub-jects being oriental women, gardens of love, and similar themes. The few landscapes we can date accurately to that period (*Cattle in the Forest of Fontainebleau* of 1846, in the Louvre) are very close to Rousseau. *Descent of the Bohemians* (No. 38) of 1844 has most of the elements of Diaz' work of the forties together in the one composition. The land-scape is richly painted, with the interest in varied textures so strong that no sky shows. Any one figure or any group of two or more can be found in separate paintings; even the dogs were often given their own composition. The pure landscapes, by which we now remember Diaz, became a major part of his output only after 1848, but his figure studies of the forties had a most profound influence on later art. Diaz drew together several cur-rents (Correggio, Titian, Boucher, Prud'hon and Delacroix) centering on the nude and clothed female placed out-of-doors, and passed them on to other artists. Couture, Millet and Daubigny, in his rare figure paintings, fell under his spell shortly after 1840; Cour-bet's *Demoiselles des bords de la Seine* of 1856 and his forest interiors with nudes or hunters (for Diaz also was fond of this theme) cannot be properly understood unless we study Diaz' work. His most direct heir of a subsequent generation was Monticelli, but both Renoir and Fantin-Latour found Diaz an important graft on the tree of their heritage. The ten paintings he exhibited in the Salon of 1847, two landscapes, one paint-ing of dogs, seven of nymphs and bathers, are a token of his established place on the eve of the Revolution.

Millet

Millet divided his time from 1840 to 1844 between Paris and Cherbourg then, following a year in Le Havre, he settled in Paris and remained there through the Revolution. Until about 1846, portraits were his chief means of livelihood (fifty-two portraits in oils sur-vive from the years before 1847), together with paintings and pastels close to Diaz in both style and subject. Twenty-five nudes in oils, plus the many *scènes galantes*, pastels and drawings, make of Millet a major artist of the female, second only to Diaz himself.

It is elsewhere that we find the signs of the future, for all that. Two currents within his work eventually lead to his famous paintings of rural life. One is the arcadian tradi-tion represented more importantly by Corot, bucolic shepherds and shepherdesses, or antique rural deities that come from Virgil and Theocritus by way of the Claudesque. These begin about 1842 and extend through 1847; they continue beyond that date, but modified by a naturalism that supplants the Diaz manner. The second type, which begins about 1844, is a more robust one stemming from the "strong" artists, Michelangelo, Poussin and the Spanish. All of the subjects are contemporary in feeling: distraught fishermen's families, homeless wanderers, occasional peasants and city-dwellers at work. The earlier of this sort have a choppy brushstroke and varied color; the later ones a smoother, liquid stroke and a more limited palette. Because the two overlap, it is impossible to say that *Les Errants* (No. 61) comes after *The Quarriers* (No. 59), but in any case they represent the two sides of the style, and from them will spring his first well-known paintings. No landscapes before 1848 can be identified. He was by 1847 a friend of the other Barbizon artists, but his art originated in a separate mold and will be a new factor in the fifties.

The Revolution of 1848

A CURIOUS, if logical, corollary of our modern concern for the purely formal qualities of art has been to deny the significance of "message," morality and the social correlatives of past art, but if we were to set aside the social history of the mid-century in France, we could not understand its art. Although the years 1830 to 1885 form one integral period in the evolution of landscape, the Revolution of 1848 is a major dividing line. It marks the end of Romanticism and the triumph of naturalism among progressive artists and critics. The years before 1848, as far as landscape alone is concerned, are a preparation for what follows, and what was an art strongly laced with Romanticism becomes one in which Romantic feelings, though still in evidence, take second place. But 1848 marks the beginning of something entirely new: naturalism in figure painting. A study of the visual arts alone could not possibly explain the pulling together of so many diverse currents after 1848. While we should avoid the view that art mirrors society (only bad art does), we must understand that it interacts with social currents.

The Growth of Social Consciousness

The Salon of 1831 was characterized by Decamps' *The Turkish Patrol*, Devéria's *The Oath of Louis-Philippe*, Delacroix' *Liberty leading the People*, an allegorical rather than a naturalistic painting, and Huet's *Sun setting behind an old abbey*. Rousseau's painting of the Auvergne and Corot's of Fontainebleau had more of the future landscape in them, but were quite Romantic in conception. The Salon of 1848, by contrast, was characterized not just by a greatly expanded section of landscape, including many now frankly naturalistic in feeling, but also by a sudden flowering of scenes of daily life in city and country: a winnower by Millet, an interior of a forge by Bonhommé, a group of miners by Loubon, rural interiors by Lambert, a woman churning butter by Hébert, and similar motifs by Antigua, Bonvin, Cals, Chaplin, Feyeu, Frère, Jeanron, Luminais. . . .

What had happened in these few years? Simply stated, the radical art of 1831, allied to the July Monarchy, was Romantic, whereas the radical art of 1848, allied to the Republic, was naturalistic. In the intervening years there had been a steady growth of a new social consciousness as the middle class came into full power, concomitant with the dying gasps of the aristocracy and theocracy which had ruled the pre-modern era. Those grouped around Saint-Simon and Comte, Louis Blanc, Michelet and the Fouriéristes called for an art of actuality as a means of communicating with the masses, who were to be thus educated to inherit the power and knowledge of the moribund elite. At first their concept of an art of actuality was heavily tinged with Romanticism, but moral and social truth gradually became synonymous with contemporary life, an evolution one finds in the writings of Rousseau's friend Thoré, Alexandre Decamps or Charles Blanc.

A sense of naturalism or realism (both terms were in use by the early thirties) also developed independently of radical social thought. We have seen that from the late twenties, landscape artists studied directly from nature although their Salon pictures were still studio compositions closer to the grand tradition. One major characteristic of landscape was its depiction of the regions of France, a kind of native realism given the fact that Italy was heretofore the proper subject for landscape. Rousseau, Corot and the others traversed the country, their paintings picking out particular qualities of each region, parallel to the travel books which mushroomed in the same period, illustrated by Daubigny, Jacque and others. Many of the landscapes showed peasant life, if in small scale. The Leleux brothers were the best known of many who featured the regional peasantry; Daumier, Cals and Jeanron were among those who portrayed the life of the humble dwellers of the city.

The strongest evidence for a growth of social consciousness is found in literature. Rural genre was already important in the thirties, and grew apace: Balzac, Gautier, Lamartine ("Jocelyn, "1856) and George Sand. In "Valentine" of 1832, Mme. Sand began her celebration of the rural life of her native Berry, a region favored also by Rousseau and Dupré, who were her friends. Gautier in the thirties wrote poems of rural life and, despite his position as the arch-defender of art for art's sake, he wrote in his Salon of 1846 that "The glorification of man and of the beauties of nature, that would seem to be the goal of art in the future." As in painting, modern life meant rural life, and city themes were less common for reasons we will examine later. With the release of the human spirit in 1848, and coincident with the sudden prominence of Millet and Courbet, a whole literature of country life came into vogue. Pierre Dupont, a friend of Champfleury, Courbet's defender, and of George Sand, published "Les Paysans" in 1846 and "Chants rustiques" three years later. By 1848 he was established as one of the chief attractions in the artistic circles of Paris, and remained so for some time. Throughout his life Daubigny sang Dupont's songs with gusto. Unlike Balzac's gross peasants of mean and savage temper, Dupont's are matter-of-fact. In his songs and poems there are most of the themes that Millet would shortly be painting. Courbet's childhood friend Max Büchon not only wrote of rural life, he also translated the rustic poetry of Hebel, Auerbach, Gotthelf and others in the wake of the 1848 upheaval. It is no surprise that in 1850, the literary and artistic group led by Champfleury and Courbet included Castagnary, Dupont, Mathieu, Bonvin and occasionally Corot and Daumier.

The Revolution of 1848 brought all these currents together, joining the political and the artistic. The artists had already been waging a battle with the Academy and the Salon, and some of their efforts went as far as the legal incorporation of an independent group in Barye's studio in April, 1847, which involved Scheffer, Delacroix, Decamps, Dupré, Rousseau, Jacque, Daumier and Jeanron. The artists linked their professional aspirations with the social and political ideals of 1848, because artist and radical had a common enemy. After the February insurrection, Charles Blanc was made director of the fine arts, Jeanron (a friend of most of the Barbizon artists and of Louis Blanc, whose "Histoire de dix ans" he illustrated) head of the national museums, and Ledru-Rollin, Minister of the Interior. As a result of their progressive direction, state commissions were awarded Millet, Rousseau, Daubigny and Dupré. The ferment in the spring of 1848 brought artists into the realm of political action in other ways. Rousseau's friend Thoré founded the "Vraie République" with the aid of George Sand, Barbès and Pierre Leroux, that old Saint-Simoniste; Millet, Diaz and Daumier competed (unsuccessfully) for a figure of the Republic; the artists won their cherished goal, a jury-free Salon, and Corot, Rousseau and Dupré were members of the managing committee; Rousseau, Diaz and Dupré were active in the artists' section for the constituent assembly; Diaz was a member of an official delegation of artists to the government. Daubigny, Diaz and Troyon were Republicans of long standing, and so were Millet, Rousseau, Dupré and Jacque, all of whom fought on the barricades in June.

If we needed further proof of the interlocking of art and social events, we could find it even outside the Barbizon group. For example, Lowlands art, which had been of such importance since 1830, was discovered in 1848 to be an art of the common people. As such it was associated thereafter with the work of Courbet, Millet, Dupont and Mathieu. Their defenders sung their praises because of it, and their enemies decried it. Partisans of the grand tradition and members of the alliance of aristocracy and upper middle class attacked Courbet and Millet for their socialistic art, automatically linking motifs of everyday life with radical political convictions. During the heyday of the Revolution, other painters of the humble people were celebrated, among them Chardin and the Le Nain brothers. They were included in the third exhibition of the Association des Artistes in 1848, along with Corot, Dupré and Rousseau. In the same year the Louvre's paintings by the Le Nain were brought to honored places in the exhibition rooms, and in 1850 they were revived in full force in an important article by Champfleury.

The Barbizon Artists

Not only did the Barbizon artists participate in the events of 1848, their very careers were affected and, in some cases, literally given shape by the Revolution. Without the free juries they had helped win for the Salons of 1848 and 1849, they would have suffered the exclusion which warped the public knowledge of Rousseau after 1836. The pre-1848 Salon never would have accepted their paintings—at least not the same ones. Daumier had the courage to exhibit in the Salon for the first time in 1849. Corot was inspired in the same year to show a study from nature (*The Colisseum* of 1827, in the Louvre), something he had never before done, and in 1852, his first plein-air painting of a French site

(*Port de la Rochelle*, Yale University). Diaz began to paint pure landscapes in great numbers. Daubigny and Troyon reached their fame only after 1848. Rousseau exhibited in the Salon of 1849 for the first time since 1836 and was at last widely accepted. Dupré retired to l'Isle-Adam, a confirmation of the same general phenomenon because he had been moving toward isolation and away from naturalism, and apparently could not weather the triumph of the new art. Jacque and Millet also left Paris, thanks to Millet's generous government commission (another specific link with the events of 1848), and settled in Barbizon. Millet not only achieved notoriety, but he forsook his styles and subjects of the forties for a devotion to rural genre and to landscape, which was utterly new in his art.

It is true that the public acclaim of naturalism lasted a short time. The June Days of 1848 already marked the downfall of the Revolution, and the Republic only staggered along for four years. When the Second Empire was declared, the radical spirit in government was replaced by the old school, and official recognition of the Barbizon artists was weakened. Nonetheless, all of them except Millet had found a permanent body of patrons, including Napoleon III, and all that was vital in French art centered around the victorious naturalism of Courbet and the painters of Barbizon.

1848–1863

WHEN we look back on the fifteen years preceding the appearance of Manet, we think of the Barbizon artists, their allies Jongkind and Boudin, and Courbet. Despite the fact that they represented the progressive art of the period, other artists were more acceptable to their contemporaries and should be kept in mind as a foil for the study of their painting. Delacroix and Ingres maintained their positions as leaders of the opposed camps of Romanticism and Classicism. Among the artists lionized by the court and the public were Horace Vernet, a battle painter, Meissonier, a genre specialist, Fromentin, an orientalist, Winterhalter and Stevens, society portraitists. The most prominent younger painters who became famous in these years were Gérome, Cabanel, Bouguereau and Baudry. Naturalism was still so little palatable to the Academy that in the Salon of 1863, the main exhibition room was given over entirely to battle scenes and society portraits.

Once below the surface, however, we discover that by 1863 all of the Barbizon artists were well enough appreciated to have found financial success. A second generation had already entered the Salon: Chintreuil, Ménard, Français, Lépine, and artists like Rosa Bonheur or Jules Breton, painters of animals and peasants, had won considerable reputations. Concurrently, the expansion of dealers' activities provided new outlets for exhibition. Louis Martinet's exhibitions on the boulevards beginning in 1860 featured the work of the Barbizon artists, and Durand-Ruel, Petit and other dealers were organizing more frequent public shows. The year 1863, when works by Courbet, Manet, Whistler, Jongkind and Fantin-Latour were rejected by the Salon, seemed at the time a triumph for the art of Cabanel, Baudry and Amaury-Duval (all three exhibited Venuses). The rejected artists had to exhibit in the Salon des Réfusés, which the conservatives believed would drown the exhibitors in ridicule. On the contrary, this exhibition, the result of artists' endeavors to win a jury-free Salon that had begun in the thirties, proved ultimately to be the consummation of the split between progressive and academic art. To be sure, the Impressionists for many years yet tried to win entry to the Salon, but henceforth progressive art made its way to the public in independent exhibitions, while the official art of the Salon foundered and gradually died.

Courbet

The most notorious artist after 1848 was Courbet and he was, willy-nilly, associated by the public with the Barbizon artists. Beginning with his *Stonebreakers* and his *Burial at Ornans* in the Salon of 1850–51, he regularly assaulted the public with controversial paintings which gave him the honor of being the most conspicuous painter alive. His historical role was to focus attention upon realism in art. It had been a major aspect of Barbizon art since the thirties, but had never been brought so distinctly to the fore. Courbet might seem to have arisen independently of the Barbizon school, but he was indebted to them in the formation of his art. His *Vintage at Ornans* (O. Reinhart) in the Salon of 1849 is close to Rousseau's and Dupré's style of the forties, and his *Meuse River at Freyr* (Lille) of about 1851 is just as close to Rousseau's paintings of the Auvergne. The left-hand figure of the famous *Stonebreakers* (Dresden) in the Salon of 1850–51 is Millet's *Winnower* of 1848, turned to a three-quarters view. Even more surprising is the fact that his *Spinner Asleep* (Montpellier) of 1853 is a virtual copy of a Millet dating from 1846 (collection unknown). Such comparisons, of course, are not intended to describe Courbet as a derivative artist, but to call attention to his real position as a participant in the currents of art which are our central theme.

Millet

From the time his *Sower* (No. 63) appeared in the same Salon with the *Stonebreakers*, Millet was coupled with Courbet as a socialist revolutionary. The mere fact that he painted peasants was enough to raise fears of 1848 in the bourgeois critics. Besides, peasants were not noble figures and hence not fit subjects for art. There was indeed a certain logic to these accusations. Millet was a fatalist, the opposite of a revolutionary, but his roots were in the social consciousness of the 1848 days. Not only did he show that common life and work were, in fact, noble, but also he preached a moral lesson. His figures implied that the work of the poor is morally superior to traditional themes from history, mythology and religion. Hence for the bourgeoisie his *Sower* was casting the seeds of revolution, his *Gleaners* were "the three fates of pauperism," and his *Man with a Hoe* was dubbed "Dumoulard," the name of a field worker who had murdered his employer's family. Millet managed nonetheless to make a living. He was selling his drawings in quantity by 1851; and in 1853 all of his Salon pictures were bought by Americans (William Hunt and Martin Brimmer; all three paintings now in the Museum of Fine Arts, Boston); by 1863

41

his fortunes had so improved he was thereafter comfortably off. Despite a few rejections, he exhibited regularly in the Salons and, from 1860, found a ready outlet for his paintings in dealers' exhibitions. He was first accepted abroad, in Holland, Great Britain and America, where his fame was spread by several Americans who became his disciples: Hunt, Babcock and Edward Wheelwright.

When Millet settled in Barbizon in 1849, he found an escape from the city he had grown to detest. He wrote to a friend in 1851,

> If you could only see how beautiful the forest is! I run over there sometimes at the end of the day, when my work is done, and I return each time, crushed. There is a calmness, of a terrible grandeur, so much so that I surprise myself being really afraid. I don't know what those fellows, the trees, are saying to each other; but they're saying something we don't understand, because we don't speak the same language.

At first he carried with him the passions of the Revolutionary period, and until about 1854, even his peaceful scenes are full of a strength at times heroic, at times bordering on violence. Laundresses at work or faggot gatherers adopt Michelangelesque positions, their bodies twisted and their muscles taut. Single figures like *The Sower* strike bold poses as they stride across the earth. Landscapes are full of the melancholy of loneliness and nighttime (No. 64). His figure style merges two currents, the tradition of antique sculpture, Michelangelo and Poussin, and the Dutch genre tradition seen through the eyes of Chardin. *Harvesters Resting* (Museum of Fine Arts, Boston) of the 1853 Salon has a group of seated figures in a powerful sculptural style which prompted one critic to call him a "rustic Michelangelo." His many interiors, like *The Spinner* (No. 65), recall instead Dutch genre and Chardin, while guarding an epic nobility. Drawings of the same years show more clearly than the paintings his origins in the arcadian. The shepherdesses and cowherds are naturalistic heirs of Virgil and Theocritus, whom he loved (he was an accomplished Latinist), and are related also to Corot's bucolic figures of the previous decade.

Millet's *Man Grafting a Tree* (formerly Rockefeller collection) of 1855 announced a new phase in his art. The calm he had come to seek finally subdued the passions of his early peasant themes. Instead of a Michelangelesque energy, his peasant has a noble simple pose; the woman holds their child in her arms as she stands, like a stately Roman matron, watching her husband. The two figures are aligned along a frontal plane, the compositional scheme which Millet used for two of his most famous pictures, *The Gleaners* of 1857 and *The Angelus* of 1859. Far from being naturalistic in detail, the figures in all three paintings are rendered with a solid economy that derives from classical relief sculpture. Some of his contemporaries realized that he approached rural life not directly, but through the Western pictorial tradition and classical literature. *Man Grafting* reminded them of Virgil's famous verse, *Insere, Daphne, piros; carpent tuo poma nepotes*: "Graft pear trees, Daphnis, posterity shall pluck thy fruit." In the juxtaposition of man grafting tree and his wife holding their baby, there is an obvious allegory which shows how little the artist was interested in merely reproducing scenes from na-

38   DIAZ.   *Descent of the Bohemians* (Bohémiens se rendant à une fête). 1844

ture. Millet is a painter in the classical tradition. Unlike Rousseau, so wrapped up in the fleeting aspects of nature, he created types. Both his human figures and their natural environment have a feeling of permanence, because he wished to raise them above the petty details of present life and link them with the eternal peasant he found in the Bible and in classical literature.

One of the most controversial and famous paintings in Western art, *Man with a Hoe* (No. 70), originated in the same spirit. Millet said that he intended to depict the resigned, animal-like peasant who had to earn his living by the sweat of his brow, who had always done so since Biblical times. In his eternal, brutalized existence, Millet found the true primitive, a socially-conscious version of Jean-Jacque Rousseau's nature-being, in contrast to the sweet rustic of Romantic genre. His fatalism, with its moralizing overtones, has a number of sources. One of them is his temperament, melancholy by nature, which naturally led him to severe moods.

> The gayest thing I know is this calm, this silence which one enjoys so deliciously either in the forest, or in the tilled fields . . . You'll admit that this is always dream-like, and of a sad reverie, although delicious. You're seated under some trees, feeling all the goodness and tranquility that one can enjoy; you see coming out of a little path a poor figure laden with faggots. The always unexpected and striking manner in which this figure appears to you carries you away involuntarily toward the sad human condition, fatigue . . . In the cultivated places, although at times in regions hardly at all tillable, you see figures spading or hoeing; you see one, from time to time, straighten up his back . . . and wipe his forehead with the back of his hand. *You will eat your bread by the sweat of your brow.* Is that the gay, jolly work which certain people would have you believe? It is nonetheless there that I find true humanity, the great poetry.

He was fond of that other fatalist, La Fontaine, from whom he drew a number of his paintings, and quite as naturally was intrigued by German and Lowlands art of the sixteenth and seventeenth centuries, whose peasants are forebears of his exhausted, almost bestial woodcutter or man resting on his hoe. It is this constant presence of moral judgment that led people to believe Millet was religious, although he was an agnostic. He was a kind of visionary, and he elaborated an evangel which gave a view of life to an entire half-century. But he was religious in the Protestant sense, a giver of morals. His *New-Born Calf* (Chicago) of 1864, for example, was an allegory of the birth of Christ; like Van Gogh later, he believed that one must paint the *doctrine* of Christ, which he accepted as a humanitarian truth, not scenes from His life.

Millet's fatalism must also be seen as a rejection of modern urban values, another reason why critics were so short-sighted when they attacked him as a revolutionary. For Millet the most meaningful struggle in life was the peasant's battle with refractory nature, not the urban worker's with social forces. It was *because* he was fully conscious of the dramatic upheavals being wrought in the urban-industrial revolution that he fled Paris for Barbizon. He had lived the better part of twelve years in the capital; he was the most erudite artist of his generation, who could cite from memory Burns, Milton, Dante, Shakespeare, La Fontaine, Virgil, Theocritus, the Bible. He was not a peasant simply painting other peasants, as was long believed, but a most cultured man who looked at the people of the soil from a great height. He found them survivors of ancient times, still living crudely as slaves to natural forces, because he wanted the certainty of contact with the past. He needed to embrace with fervor that side of life which was untouched by the modern world, in opposition to which he set himself.

> I insist on giving her [a woman carding wool] an appearance and a calm which are not possessed by the wool-carders of the suburbs.
> I intend that the beings I represent have an air of being rooted in their position, that it would be impossible to imagine that they could think of being other than they are.

In the life of Barbizon, he sought the ancient social unit of family and farm, that almost tribal entity whose breaking up he had witnessed (as in his own case!) in the migration of rural dweller to the city. Peasant art, in short, was only possible when man feared that he was losing the past. The truly contemporary phenomenon was not the rural dweller but the urban worker, just as the city was the sign of modernity, not untouched nature. Barbizon art, based upon nature and the peasant, was an impassioned outcry against the onrushing urban-industrial revolution.

Millet's most famous paintings had this moral urgency, but he also found the past in the more pleasant side of rural life. Shepherdesses guarding their flocks, cowherds returning home at dusk, milkmaids (No. 67), rabbits in the forest (No. 69) could all step from the pages of Virgil. When he had to produce Salon pictures, his moralistic inclinations got the upper hand, and his more gentle works, seldom exhibited, were overlooked. He also painted many pure landscapes, but largely after 1863. Before that date his important landscapes are in his figure compositions, but in these he helped transform the painting of nature. Millet was the first artist in the nineteenth century to give equal importance to both elements of his composition, so that his landscapes produced a new type of figure, and his figures, a new kind of landscape. Nature and man are interdependent. Each acts on the other, neither is just an accessory as is usually the case with Corot, Daubigny or Rousseau. His man with a hoe must hack away at the soil, which obdurately resists his labors, and each has the same exhausted character. Instead of the spatial wedge, carefully framed by trees, which Rousseau favored, Millet opened out his spaces as he reached for the vastness of nature, which spread beyond his frame to suggest its infinitude. In many early works, *The Sower*, for example, man makes his eternal gesture against a hillside, whose high horizon evokes the rotundity of the globe. "I love," he wrote Rousseau, "the delicious silhouette of a human marching so solemnly on the heights . . . and many other things [instead of] the noise of the wheels of an omnibus or the 'music' of a tinker."

By the mid-fifties, the plains of Barbizon replaced the hills of Cherbourg, but there is the same universality. He generalized the flatlands of Brie as Poussin did the Roman Campagna. In contrast to Rousseau, so concerned with the particulars of weather and time, he had a predilection for the classical four seasons of the year, and he characterized them not alone by the state of nature, but by the human labors typical of those seasons. After 1863, pure landscape came to dominate Millet's art, partly a result of his long association with Rousseau, but he always retained the sense of nature altered by man's labor.

Daubigny

Daubigny kept up his graphic work after the Revolution, but he was able to devote the bulk of his time to painting and exhibited in the Salon until his death. A government purchase in 1852 followed by the Emperor's acquiring his *Pond of Gylieu* (No. 23) the next year secured his reputation and lifted him above financial want. He travelled more extensively, especially to Optevoz and the Isère district, and to Villerville on the Channel coast. In 1860 he settled permanently in Auvers, the region near Paris that he had favored above all others.

In the sudden expansion of his activity as a painter after 1848, he at first continued in a Claudesque manner. Then, about 1851, his major paintings began to lose their soft textures and contrived compositions, apparently because he drew closer to Dutch art and to Courbet. His compositions remained panoramic, but less obviously architectural, and his brushwork became thicker and fresher at the same time. *The Sluice at Optevoz* (Rouen), an important picture of 1855, has the palette knife textures of Courbet's Ornans landscapes. *The Mill at Optevoz* of 1857 (No. 22), however, is virtually the last major painting in which we find the heavy palette.

By that year Daubigny's art undergoes its last major transformation. The broad and liquid palette gives way to freer and smaller brushstrokes, applied more rapidly, and to lighter colors. The new style, which was the basis for the further development of his art, had been carried on parallel to the heavy manner, but in a minor key. Perhaps his growing friendship with Corot fortified his resolve to diminish the studio component of his finished works, and to increase the quality of fresh study from nature. Other indications of the same direction are his annual trips to the Channel coast beginning in 1854, and the launching of his studio-boat in 1857. He discovered that the moist luminosity of the seacoast and the river-basins near Paris required him to flood his canvases with lighter tones, and that they had to be brushed more quickly in order to capture the constantly changing conditions inherent in such humid regions. From this time forward, water was to be his constant theme, no longer wooded glades or the calm ponds and rivers of southern France, and his only important trips abroad were to London and Holland, Northern maritime countries.

1857 is also the year in which these characteristics of Daubigny's art, so important for Impressionism, were underscored by his critics. His friend and disciple, Frédéric Henriet, published in "l'Artiste" that year a ringing defence of Daubigny (undoubtedly written with the artist's knowledge), in which he listed three prime attributes. One is "sincerity," by which he meant that Daubigny was faithful first to his feelings of nature. "He copies nature with his soul . . . The model is before his eyes, but it is in his heart that he finds the exquisite feeling with which he impregnates his work." This phrase recalls Zola's famous dictum applied to the Impressionists, "nature seen through a temperament," and points out once again that naturalism did not mean a slavish copy of nature, but a felt dialectic between the artist and his subject. The second attribute Henriet gives to Daubigny is the limpid clarity of his art, achieved by means of a new luminosity rather than the traditional opposition of light and dark, which he contrasts to the sad, tormented landscapes of the Romantics. The third is Daubigny's feeling of improvisation, of the direct sketch, the "impression" which must not be lost because the early stages of the painting's genesis are the seeds of his inspiration.

This last attribute, high praise for Henriet, Pelloquet and other friendly critics, was precisely the wedge of the attacks upon Daubigny. In 1861 Gautier accused him of painting only "an impression." "Each object," he wrote, "is distinguished by a real or apparent contour, and the landscapes of M. Daubigny offer little more than a juxtaposition of spots of color." In other words, Daubigny no longer clearly separated the parts of his landscape when he replaced contours and chiaroscuro with a quasi-Impressionist luminosity. It was in this dispute, which revolved around his diminishing the difference between sketch and finished painting, that the battle for Impressionism was first engaged.

We should not, however, consider this the only side of Daubigny's art, even if it was the most important for the future. Among his paintings there were still strong echoes of Claude and the eighteenth century, while his nocturnal landscapes recall Rousseau and the more Romantic works of Corot. *Sunset on the Seine* (No. 26) of 1856 is not far removed from Corot's *Sodom* (No. 9) of a year later; his *Peasant Watering his Donkey*, a shadowy twilight scene, took its place alongside Corot's *Dante and Virgil* in the Salon of 1859.

Rousseau

After years of isolation, Rousseau rose to fame in 1849. He had more patrons than he could satisfy, and the official world finally accepted him. He shared a special room with Decamps in the Universal Exhibition of 1855. Then, about 1857, his stock began to fall and he was again in financial difficulties until the last years of his life. From 1848 to 1863 he travelled seldom, spending most of his time at Barbizon, where he lived in close friendship with Millet, who replaced Dupré (with whom he had broken in 1849).

During his period of success, Rousseau worked hard to finish paintings for his many patrons. Many of them were compositions of the forties given a final polish, with the result that they sometimes have a mechanical surface. His success gave him a tranquility he had never before enjoyed, and his style was marked by a patient inventory of nature. Whether or not it was because his market began to fail him in 1857, Rousseau began with renewed vigor to follow the two paths that characterized his work before 1848. On the one hand he turned to emotional forest sunsets (No. 100), of heightened color, stronger contrasts of hue, and more varied textures in comparison with his earlier style. On the other, he pursued his obsession with the luminosity of nature, which he painted in large and free strokes, somewhat like chopped straw (No. 98). The latter are the most original works of his later years. Through their tapestries of color, we can feel stirring the breeze of Impressionism.

59 MILLET. *The Quarriers.* c. 1846

64   MILLET. *Starry Night.* c. 1850–51

Corot

Corot's art is too well known to need much attention here, since its main directions, with the exception of the late figure pieces, were established by 1848. The exquisite paintings of single women, begun in numbers about 1856, did not enter importantly into the history of art during Corot's own lifetime; he exhibited the first one only in 1869. His Salon entries included a few landscape studies, but he maintained his allegiance to tradition in his more typical exhibition pictures: *Christ in the Garden of Olives*, *Saint Sebastian*, *Macbeth*, and a great many *Souvenirs*, *Matinées*, *Soirs*, and dancing nymphs. In these, especially the more robust compositions like *Sodom*, Corot remains a member of the older Romantic generation. This does not gainsay the fact that his splendid Claudesque landscapes (*Souvenir de Mortefontaine*, No. 16) had much to offer the Impressionists, but they preferred, as do we, his plein-air paintings. Between 1840 and 1865 his studies shed a number of Renaissance devices in favor of flatter spaces and simpler, more luminous surfaces. There are fewer zig-zag recessions, and fewer planes stationed at specific intervals in depth, like the screens of a theater décor. Instead the forms move up toward the surface and one screen, not several, often dominates the composition. It is placed close to the foreground and parallel to the picture plane, a device used commonly also in his studio paintings. In harmony with these changes, his palette, though in any one picture still restricted to a narrow tonal range, becomes even lighter and contrasts of light and dark are subdued.

Troyon

If we were to use the popular, but erroneous yardstick of an artist's influence to judge his merits, we would probably have to conclude that Troyon was the greatest of the Barbizon painters. When he turned to animal painting upon his return from Holland, he won instantaneous success. By 1855 there were little Troyons in the Salons and exhibitions throughout the Lowlands and Germany. By 1860 his influence was so pervasive that an entire generation of followers, equalled only by Millet's of a few years later, was coming to maturity.

He exhibited his first animal painting in the Salon of 1849, and until 1852 his style was laced with direct borrowings from Cuyp, Potter and other Dutch painters. During his long campaign in Normandy in 1852, he at last found himself. He assimilated the Dutch style with his own studies of nature, developing a painterly style of surprising energy. The interaction of animal and landscape, due to his long apprenticeship as a landscape painter, is his special quality. The cows and trees of *Pasture in Normandy* (No. 105) seem to be equally pensive; the animals' bodies have matte and humid surfaces in keeping with the moist Norman sky. When he paints a storm (*The Bull, Stormy Weather* of 1850–52, in the Louvre), his bull leans to one side to fortify the imbalance in nature. The approaching storm of *The Pointer* (No. 106) is matched by the tense dog poised expectantly like the rolling rainclouds above.

Because we tend to look at Troyon through the eyes of his many followers, we find it hard to acknowledge his worth. The imitators have beclouded the original. In his pure landscapes there is no such problem. *Le Tréport* (No. 107) is typical of the late seascapes whose variety and delicacy tell us why Corot advised Boudin to work with him.

1864–1878

THE TWILIGHT of Barbizon art was not a period of sadness and decay. It is epitomized instead by Rousseau who, as he lay paralyzed and dying in his house in Barbizon, managed with his one good arm to drag himself up so that he could see the tops of poplar trees from his window. These curious drawings of just the tops of trees have the passion of a vital old age, still lusty enough to contain the seeds of a young art, Impressionism. Troyon died in 1865, and Rousseau two years later. Millet, Corot and their friend Barye died in 1875, and before four years had passed, nearly the entire generation had been wiped out in the successive deaths of Diaz, Courbet, Daubigny and Daumier. Only Dupré and Jacque survived beyond this time. But between 1864 and 1878, Barbizon art had a grand late flowering.

Rousseau

In 1864, Rousseau had only three more years to live, but he was struggling with an entirely new problem. Sometime before the spring of 1863 he had discovered Japanese prints and drawings. It has proved impossible to verify the story that Bracquemond had an album of Hokusai drawings in 1856, but in that year three "facsimiles" of Japanese drawings were published in the popular "Magasin Pittoresque," and interest in the newly discovered art slowly grew. By 1864 Millet and Rousseau were rivalling each other in collecting the colored prints from Japan. Rousseau was thrown into a crisis by them. In 1863 he repainted entirely the *Village of Becquigny* (Frick Collection) that had been on his easel since 1857, and had to suffer the attacks of his friends who found disagreeable the sudden incursion of flatness and the hot atmosphere of the East into a painting of the humid village of Picardie.

Before he died, Rousseau was over his first infatuation with Japanese art and restored the painting to its native climate, but when it was exhibited in 1864 it still bore the marks of a new manner. Even his friend Castagnary could not accept the trees "plastered like a fan against the sky" and most of the critics attacked his lack of modelling. Today we find the Japanese phase only in a few drawings and unfinished sketches. *La Futaie du Bois de Macherin, Barbizon*, reproduced in the Amand-Durand album of 1873, has a remarkable flatness and the sinuous arabesques of Japanese art. But by late 1865 Rousseau had weathered the crisis and the chief residue was a slight simplification of contour, a greater flatness of foliage, and a heightened color. All of these were tendencies in his art before 1862, so that for Rousseau, the first major artist to be influenced by Japanese prints, Eastern art was a catalyst in an indigenous development.

Millet

As if to prove that prosperity need not mean the diluting of art, and that obscurity is not always the mother of the most creative work, Millet used his new-found success after 1863 to produce a remarkable series of pastels, drawings and paintings. He had from youth worked in pastels, but never with the concentration of the years 1865 to 1869. *Meridian* (No. 71) is probably early in the series, because the chalk is laid down rather thickly and the colors are mixed with black. By 1868 (*Farmyard in Winter*, No. 74) he no longer used pastel as though it were paint, but stroked the surface delicately, letting his tinted paper show through. He also used the most intense colors available whenever the subject permitted. The pastels of the late sixties, ranging widely in subject from figure composition to landscape, from the Auvergne to Brie, from colorful spring to dour winter, are Millet's greatest works. His special gift was drawing, and in pastel he could draw directly in color to exploit the best of both.

Until his death he continued to draw in black and white, not just to serve his pastels and paintings, but for its own sake. *Twilight* (No. 72), touched lightly with colored chalks, has a quality we tend to associate first with Seurat, partly because he drew inspiration from such drawings in developing his own shadowy style. Millet cherished the hours of twilight which suited his introspective nature and gave him an excuse to build his forms with pools of darkness and delicate greys. A new and opposed type of drawing appeared in the same years. *Un Sentier* (No. 73) is one of the lovely ink drawings of the environs of Vichy, where Millet spent a few weeks in the early summers of 1866, 1867 and 1868. In contrast to his landscape drawings of the fifties, which are quite dense and rich, the Vichy drawings of 1866 have an elegant lightness which results from Millet's study of Japanese prints and drawings. The high horizon line, firm arabesques and absence of modelling reflect Eastern art, and are parallel to the intensifying of his palette in both oils and pastels.

In addition to the wonderful sequence of pastels and the new style in landscape drawing, there are two further shifts in Millet's work after 1863, one concerning figure composition, the other, landscape. In 1869 he returned to painting as his major occupation and until 1874 devoted himself to about forty large oils. *Buckwheat Harvest* (No. 76), "summer" of the four seasons begun in 1858 for the collector Hartmann, has an exquisite palette dominated by the purples of buckwheat hulls, but its most remarkable feature is the drawing of the figures. We are reminded of Van Gogh not just because of the style, but because in the drawing we feel a similar tragic emotion. The vigorous, angular drawing of the two women in the foreground, not entirely covered by the paint, records Millet's seizing upon the age-old harvest rite as a way of making contact with the permanence of time.

In the extraordinary *Birdnesters* (No. 78) there are other ties to the past. Millet may have been thinking of the battles of pygmies and cranes on Greek vases, since the Norman activity carried on the ancient killing of birds either for food or to prevent their attacking grainfields. There is little doubt that he was conscious of wedding the past with the present in such a picture. He was fond of the "primitive" artists, and owned reproductions of Giotto and Fra Angelico. The blocky peasants of *Birdnesters* have something of the quattrocento about them—Masaccio, Fra Angelico, Gozzoli—as well as of Bruegel.

The pastel *Meridian* has a similar chunkiness of form and is another of the works of Millet's late years that shares in his creation of a new primitivism.

It is in landscape that the most sweeping changes occur after 1863. Before that date he completed relatively few major landscapes, but afterwards he made it his first love. Unlike Rousseau, who preferred the solitude of forest or marshy plain, Millet painted fields and hills which bore the effects of man's labor, and in them he found all the variety of passion or reverie that he felt in humankind. Some of them can only be called "moral landscapes." *Winter, the Crows* of 1862–67 (Vienna), of which Van Gogh made a copy, *November* of 1870 (Berlin) and *Le Coup de Vent* of 1873 (Cardiff) are steeped in a blustery, wintry sadness that judges us, the observers, as though the abandoned harrows, gaunt trees and fluttering crows were challenging us to remember that one day we, too, would be spent and exhausted by constant toil.

The great brooding landscapes are not as common in Millet's later painting as more restful compositions in which he created a sense of contentment and peaceful longing for the simple beauties of a past era. *Normandy Pasture* (No. 81) benefited from the heightened palette of the pastel period and the lightness of the Vichy drawings. The high horizon lets the forms rise up on the surface, where the broad and simple planes gently push the tremulous dabs of color into our vision. *The Church at Gréville* (No. 80) has the same air of rootedness. "The countryside here," he wrote in 1871 of his native Cherbourg region, "is truly impressive and has many characteristics of former times. One could believe himself (if he wished to avoid certain modernities) in the time of old Bruegel [le vieux Breughel]. Many villages remind one of those represented on old tapestries. The beautiful, velvety greenswards!" In some of his late landscapes, Millet went so far as to mix sand with his pigments to give a sense of the aged textures of stone. In *The Church at Gréville*, the feeling of the "time of old Bruegel" is given by the matte textures of the building which even in shadow are composed of separate hues interlocked like the weave of tapestry.

Daubigny

Millet had a profound influence on Seurat, Pissarro and Van Gogh, who were sensitive to his moral commitment, but it was Daubigny who could speak to Monet, Sisley and Renoir precisely because he had no such wells of self-judgment. He was closer to the young painters than Corot, who was always a painter of the classical school, and continued to send subject pictures to the Salon. Daubigny was a painter of pure landscape, and more devoted to plein-air painting than any other artist of his generation. Furthermore, whereas Corot's style in his studies from nature was typified by broad, relatively uniform surfaces of restricted tonal harmonies, Daubigny used a small, choppy brushstroke and a much wider choice of hue. For this reason Corot found his *Fields in the Month of June* (No. 34) too free and loose.

After 1863, Daubigny steadily narrowed the gap between his impressionistic studies and his finished works. According to his disciple Henriet, his large *Villerville-sur-mer* (Mesdag Museum) in the Salon of 1864 was done from beginning to end out-of-doors,

70   MILLET.   *Man with a Hoe.*   1859–62

100   ROUSSEAU.   *Sunset near Arbonne.* c. 1865

making it the first such major painting to be exhibited. Presumably most of his Salon pictures were not finished at the site, but they display a progressive freshness that is only exceeded by his smaller pictures, of which *The Dunes* (No. 31) and *The Beach at Villerville* (No. 35) are among the most superb.

Diaz

It would be shocking even to think of Diaz growing weaker with old age—that one-legged *bon vivant* who had piped his way through life like a gypsy. A tireless worker to the end, he was utterly devoid of the moralizing of Millet and Rousseau, and equally immune to the melancholy of Corot and Daubigny. He was a painter's painter and a charmer's charmer. Probably the truest revelation of his character are his gypsies, harem girls and nymphs who continued to people his canvases up to his death. Because of the overweening importance of landscape after the mid-century, his later figure compositions are ignored, although they are as numerous as his landscapes and had some importance for Corot's paintings of women, for Renoir, Monticelli and a number of Italian followers. He is remembered instead for his sparkling forests and meadows, whose unique quality is their lustrous surfaces. They sprang fully developed about 1850 from his style of the forties. During the fifties (*Forest of Fontainebleau*, No. 41) his modelling tended to be rather solid and his spaces well defined, but he gradually expanded his style in two complementary directions. One, more commonly his forest interiors, established a dark matrix of russet and golden browns on which he superimposed small dabs of Rembrandtesque gold, silver, white, yellow and orange. These are loosely handled and no longer produce a very tangible roundness or solidity in the individual forms. Sometimes they are pushed to an extreme and the flecks of pigment float on the surface like phosphorescent tones in a nocturnal sea. The other direction, usually in his open meadows, has a much lighter tonality, almost fluffy (*Valley Marsh*, No. 44). In both cases he mixed hardly any oil with his pigments, but applied them directly, using a palette knife, then went over the surface with dilute glazes. The glazes, and the final coat of varnish, act as a translucent layer through which the color is refracted, heightening their shimmer. It was because he was a painter of the visual rather than the sculptural surface that he had such significance for Renoir and the other Impressionists.

The Meaning of Barbizon Art

THE PURELY HISTORICAL treatment of art is bloodless. The real heritage of Barbizon art is in the paintings, and their vitality must be experienced in our viscera. Otherwise works of art are documents to be assessed, catalogued and filed away. But there is a proper use of history, namely, to prod us into discoveries which release our imaginations and permit us to rise to the realm of true *poesis*. An historical evaluation of Barbizon art will only have value if it succeeds in doing just this.

The Fulcrum of Barbizon Art

Barbizon art was both heir and testator. It drew to itself the disparate riches of past traditions and passed them on, expanded and enriched. The process by which this was done was the creative act of the artist, one of the great treasures of humankind and one of its great enigmas. In landscape alone, the Barbizon artists melted in the crucible of their creativity five different legacies.

1. *The Anglo-Dutch.* Every Barbizon artist was a profound student of Lowlands art, and several were weaned on the English craze of 1825–35.

2. *The Classical.* Corot is the outstanding adherent of the classical tradition, but the others also assimilated the art of Poussin and Claude.

3. *The eighteenth century.* Diaz, Dupré and Troyon all began as porcelain painters, directly in the eighteenth century tradition; Corot and Daubigny were equally its heirs.

4. *The topographical and regional.* Only Millet was rooted to as few as two places, Normandy and Brie. The others adopted the fashion of travel books, some of them professionally, and broke the monopoly of Italian sites by making themselves specialists in various regions of France, with the resultant concern for the specific, no longer the general character of landscape.

5. *The plein-air.* Painting out-of-doors was altered in their hands from a custom to a necessity.

In figure painting, too, we may summarize five major traditions recast by the Barbizon artists.

1. *The Classical.* Millet was the closest student of classical sculpture and literature, but it was of significance also for Corot and Diaz.

2. *The Renaissance.* Millet was drawn especially to Michelangelo, Poussin and the Spanish; Corot, more to Leonardo and Raphael.

3. *The Rococo and arcadian.* Diaz, Millet and Corot all drank at the well of Correggio, Watteau, Boucher and Prud'hon.

4. *Genre.* All Barbizon artists fell under the sway of genre painting, represented by Lowlands artists, the Le Nain and Chardin, and all dealt in contemporary genre, even if only in small-scale figures.

5. *The "primitive."* Millet was the most absorbed in the various arts which passed for "primitive": quattrocento art in Italy, late medieval and early Renaissance prints of the North, Gothic sculpture, and Bruegel. The small figures in Rousseau's landscapes often have similar origins, and each had admitted lessons from Japanese prints and drawings by 1866.

Impressionism and Later Painting

The mid-century bequeathed this multifaceted legacy to the Impressionists. Each of the Barbizon artists had his particular qualities, but there are a number of characteristics which they shared and from which Impressionism was born. It is here that one finds the cohesiveness of the Barbizon school. Plein-air painting and the direct impression of nature are perhaps the most important. Rousseau's special easel for working out-of-doors, his and Daubigny's lean-tos, and Daubigny's studio-boat were devices to facilitate plein-air painting. In 1860, Rousseau and Ziem planned to move the Moulin de la Galette, which Ziem had bought, from Montmartre to the plains near Barbizon. By revolving the mill full circle, they would have followed the sun through the day as they painted, a project which, though abortive, is a convenient symbol for the development of later painting. Light was no less an obsession for Rousseau, Dupré, Daubigny and Corot than for Monet. Rousseau called light "the secret of Prometheus," and wrote that "without light, there is no creation, everything is chaos, death or pedantry." Plein-air painting with its fixation upon light involved another cardinal principal: the momentary effects of nature. Rousseau and Daubigny painted virtual series of the same subject under different conditions of light and weather.

The means of achieving these interlocked goals led to fundamental changes in the appearance of painting. The purely visual gradually monopolized the surface of a painting, instead of the structural. In the 1830's, the Barbizon artists were still much aware of the architecture of trees and their autonomous existence in illusionary space, but shortly after the mid-century, memory knowledge of touchable, solid masses yielded to the optical, so purged of non-visual experience that the dabs of pigment began to float free of imaginary substance. When that occurred, the artist became as much interested in the dabs as in what they represented, and by the early sixties they were all painting in a variety of small strokes whose colors, no longer blended one with another, took on new life. Earth colors, the customary matrix for brighter hues, began to wane when that matrix was no longer used, and a lighter palette was the result. Concentration on the purely visual appearance of things also produced a tendency toward greater flatness which was abetted by the choice of a narrower focal range. The Barbizon painters began to restrict their slice of nature to what the eye can see without moving back and forth, in place of the traditional panorama.

One can also distinguish the legacy of individual Barbizon artists. Corot and Daubigny were the most important for the landscape Impressionists. Corot indeed remained a vital force at the end of the century: both Seurat and Cézanne admired his sense of structure, and Puvis de Chavannes borrowed his palette and matte textures. Diaz had a veritable disciple in the person of Monticelli who, in turn, was highly regarded by Van Gogh and Cézanne. Millet's effect on Monet was only transitory, but Pissarro was his life-long heir, Seurat went through a Millet phase in the early eighties, and Van Gogh was closer to Millet than to any other of his forebears. Rousseau's studies of light and weather were basic lessons for all the Impressionists, although Cézanne was his lone spiritual legatee.

Some aspects of the Barbizon heritage are more subtle. Rousseau's struggle with the "realizing" of his "impression" was in embryo Cézanne's dilemma of "realization" and "sensation." Troyon and Millet seem the artists least likely to impress Renoir, yet his *Peasant Girl with Cow and Sheep* of 1887 (Fitzwilliam Museum), a large composition of the sour period, is right out of their work, and his young girl bending over to retrieve a croquet ball (formerly Vollard collection) is a direct transposition of one of Millet's gleaners. Pissarro's paintings in the nineties of rural markets evoke Jan Steen only because Millet had pointed the way.

Barbizon Art and the Urban-Industrial Revolution

Why is the painting of rural landscape, animals and peasants the staple of Barbizon art? For artists who professed a devotion to contemporary life, is it not paradoxical that they avoided the most contemporary phenomena, the incredible expansion of cities, the new urban populations increasingly tied to the new industry? The man of the future was the industrial worker or the middle-class manager, not the faggot-gatherer or the shepherd. The answer is so obvious that it is hard to see, like the large letters on the map in Poe's "Gold Bug." It is found already in the late eighteenth century, the very time when the urban-industrial explosion began. In his "Notes on the State of Virginia" of 1785, Thomas Jefferson proclaimed that

> Those who labour in the earth are the chosen people of God . . . Corruption of morals in the mass of cultivators is a phaenomenon of which no age nor nation has furnished an example. It is the mark set on those, who not looking up to heaven, to their own soil and industry, as does the husbandman, for their subsistence, depend for it on casualties and caprice of customers . . . While we have land to labour then, let us never wish to see our citizens occupied at a workbench, or twirling a distaff . . . let our workshops remain in Europe . . . The loss by the transportation of commodities across the Atlantic will be made up in happiness and permanence of government. The mobs of great cities add just so much to the support of pure government, as sores do to the strength of the human body.

This is the attitude of Jean-Jacques Rousseau, of Ruskin, of Delacroix, the Barbizon artists and Kropotkin. It required a century for progressive minds to look beyond the tragedy of industrialization to see its inevitability. Until the latter nineteenth century, it was still possible to believe that modern industry could be spurned, and that man could cling to the soil. Art was a century-long protest against industrialization. The Gothic and Greek revivals, like Barbizon art, were a way of pulling the mantle of the past over the ugly present. The archetypal novel plot in the nineteenth century involved a young hero who is born in the country, where he is in a state of natural grace, then goes to the city, is there corrupted, and finally is either saved or damned, be he Stendhal's Julien Sorel, Flaubert's Frédéric or Dickens' Pip. He might also be Millet, who had exactly that career. The other Barbizon artists, too, only became painters of rural nature after years in Paris. Their art must therefore be seen as a constant opposition to the city and modern life.

    1. *Opposition to the present*. "Everything I wanted to paint has been destroyed," Daubigny lamented when he went to Avalon in 1854, "trees cut down, no more water in the river, houses razed! So . . . I'm off to see if the Eternal Father hasn't upset the mountains of the Dauphiné . . ." Even in the countryside the Barbizon artists were distressed by signs of rampant change. Rousseau waged an incessant battle against the deforestation of Fontainebleau and the building of modern roads. "There is a giant which is declining; I have seen it much more beautiful, but each year they attack it, they

wound it. They have amputated his strongest branches so that the veils of the sight-seers won't get caught; they have cut his magnificent roots, to make a macadam road."

2. *Release in nature.* In all the Barbizon artists' letters, let alone their painting, the solitude, silence and peace of the country are constantly opposed to the city they had left behind. For their defenders this was one of the chief attractions of their paintings. "Daubigny's paintings," wrote Henriet in 1857, "procure for us abundantly these illusions of repose, of liberty, of solitude, which are next to happiness." We today find this equally appealing, both in their art and in our own periodic flights from the city to the country.

3. *Release in the rural past.* For these artists, the countryside was not just different from the city, it was the past still surviving in the present. Fontainebleau forest was called "Arcadia" by Rousseau, who felt that "Homer and Virgil wouldn't have disdained sitting there to muse over their poetry." Millet said that he painted his *Woman Baking Bread* (Kröller-Müller Museum) to show a ceremony that had continued unchanged for hundreds of years. He, Diaz, Corot, Rousseau and Daubigny all referred to rural life as coming from the pages of arcadian poetry.

4. *The seizing upon permanence.* Release from modern life had to provide a sense of contact with the past, rapidly slipping away, and a sense of the permanence which Jefferson, Ruskin and the others associated with the soil. Animal painting flooded the exhibition rooms of Europe and America during the early heyday of industrial expansion, when the machine would have been a more appropriate symbol of modern life. But the unchanging, unthinking brute called forth none of the associations of upheaval which the machine did. It was its very opposite. Similarly, the peasant was preferable to the urban worker. He was Jean-Jacques' and Jeffersons' primitive, untarnished by the industrial city. Even the tree becomes an image of permanence. Trees, Rousseau said, "are for me great history, that which will never change. If I could speak their language, I would be using the tongue of all ages."

5. *Melancholy and despair.* Why did the Barbizon artists ultimately fail to discover calm and release in the countryside? Of course they did at times, but most of the work of Corot and Daubigny is full of a poignant melancholy, and that of Millet and Rousseau, a more passionate despair. They could not find permanence and repose, hence their nymphs, gypsies and oriental women are alter-egos, reflecting their own wanderings over the length and breadth of France, their own sense of uprootedness. Rousseau's oak and Millet's stolid peasant did have a feeling of eternal belonging, but invested with a tragic feeling of loss. Melancholy and despair swell the pulse of their art because they were urban dwellers, who brought city attitudes with them as they attempted to seize upon nature. That hopelessness reached a climax when Van Gogh retreated from the North to Arles, when Cézanne escaped into a hermit's solitude, when Gauguin fled Western Europe entirely to seek in the Oceanic native the primitive being Millet thought he saw in the French peasant.

Naturalism

Barbizon naturalism was the chief manifestation in painting of a European-wide phenomenon of the mid-century, observable in literature and all the arts. It is not easy to define, above all in painting, because we are tempted to accept the images and think no further. Painting is a form of high poetry. Its meaning lies behind the images, just as the meaning of poetry lies behind the words. The naturalistic artist was not a kind of human watch, who merely wound up his skills and set them in motion. "True composition," wrote Rousseau, "results when the objects represented are not there for themselves, but in order to embody, under a natural appearance, the echoes they have placed in our soul." We too easily forget that one cannot copy nature. Take, for example, the effects of natural light. They must be simulated by pigments, which are opaque and dependent upon reflection; they contain no light source as does nature. Hence rays of red and green form white when they are mixed; red and green pigments form a brownish-grey. In addition, natural light has the full scale of the outdoors, painters' light is placed on a small, flat rectangle. The artist, rendered incapable of copying nature, therefore develops a whole bag of tricks which are man-made, and in the process, all his soul and being enters into his art. Naturalism is just as much a felt dialectic between the artist and nature as the most expressionistic style.

There are two poles of naturalism in Barbizon art, each conveniently represented by the two great friendships among the group. Corot and Daubigny were both painters of the countryside, Rousseau and Millet, of nature. The countryside is nature seen by a suburban stroller, which is why Corot and Daubigny were closer to Impressionism than the other two. They did not often paint forest interiors, but meadows, the environs of villages, harbors and beaches. A sense of enjoyment, a poignant enjoyment, pervades their pictures—limpid calm, gentle breaths of air, subtle harmonies of attenuated color. For all these reasons they are closer to us than Rousseau and Millet, whose different ardor we find difficult to comprehend.

Rousseau was described by Baudelaire as "tormented by a thousand devils and not knowing which one to heed." Like Millet he was devoted to the humid soil and the rough bark, to the weeds of forlorn marshes, to the lichen-covered rock. Corot and Daubigny appeal to us because they have a certain distance from the substance of nature, but Rousseau made an inventory of her riches with all the passionate exactitude of Darwin or Ruskin; he was an accomplished geologist, meteorologist and botanist. His paintings were built on a structure of hard lines, almost like engravings, because he had to have the certainty that he had penetrated to the vitals of nature. He surrounded himself with the protective embrace of writhing foliage. Most of his paintings are from the inside of the forest looking out toward the light, the opposite of Corot and Daubigny who were outside, looking in. He said that in the marsh he found the primeval ooze from which life sprang, and in the tree, the whole of past history. And always he had the convictions of a moralizer. "Do you understand now," he wrote, "that everything my intelligence reproves is in direct relation to everything my heart aspires to, and that the sight of human disdain and baseness is to me as powerful a vehicle of action in the exercise of my art as the depths of serene contemplation that I have been able to put in myself since childhood?"

Millet's naturalism is equally qualified by deep-seated emotions, and a devotion to the materiality of humble beings and substances.

> On such sad days, when the wind moans, it is grand and beautiful to walk . . . under the lofty trees denuded of their leaves, to see those poor beings twisted and tormented by the wind, left alone with the night that envelops them, and to ask yourself "What do they feel? What do they suffer?" Or, when the sun has set, to watch that afterglow in the sky, and the shadows that render objects mysteriously confused; and then follows the night, which comes brooding, dusky, silent, over this lonely country.

He was also devoted to the human being, in whose labors he saw himself. "My program is work; every man is doomed to bodily labor." His naturalism is infused with emotions bordering upon self-torture.

> Art is not a diversion, it is a conflict, a complex of wheels in which one is crushed . . . I do not wish to do away with pain, nor to find a formula that will make me stoical and indifferent. Pain is perhaps the thing that gives an artist the strongest power of expression.

It is no wonder that Van Gogh admired Millet. So far is his art from descriptive naturalism, that an Abstract Expressionist could have written the statement above.

The Meaning of Barbizon Art

Barbizon art is the result of a dialectic between the artist and nature, and will only live if we establish another, between ourselves and the paintings. We must study the paintings with at least a portion of the love with which they were created, and clear our minds of two things: a bogus historical reading, and a simplistic interpretation of naturalism. On the one hand, we must avoid seeing Barbizon art as merely the cradle of Impressionism, or as the repository of nineteenth century sentimentality. Should Millet be dismissed because of the *Angelus*? If so, then what are we to do with Lord Byron, who devoted a stanza of "Don Juan" to the same theme, beginning "Ave Maria! blessed be the hour!" and concluding "And yet the forest leaves seem'd stirr'd with prayer." This is not to deny the meaning of the associations the artist had with the objects he represented, but to suggest that we put aside conventional views and seek the answers ourselves. The process of seeking is the role of the observer, it is the way he finds in art a reality higher than the petty events of daily life. What was the plain of Barbizon before Millet painted it? What was the marsh of Berry before Rousseau transformed it by his genius?

A painting is the tangible fruit of an act of creation. "He who knows how to make something live, is God," said Rousseau. The artist finds poetry not out there somewhere, but in his soul. How easy to pass by a painting of Fontainebleau by Rousseau, but how rewarding to let him transport us to the privacy of intense artistic experience. Look at such a painting after reading his words:

One winter day I saw [this tree] covered in snow, white as one of Ossian's warriors. He spread his great arms like an old bard. A branch fell at my feet and nearly killed me; it would have been a beautiful death, in the heart of the forest, killed by an oak and perhaps forgotten there . . . See all those beautiful trees; I drew them all thirty years ago, I made all their portraits. Look at that birch over there; the sun lights it and makes of it a column of marble, a column which has muscles, limbs, hands, and a beautiful skin, white and pallid, like the skin of dryads . . . Ah! the sun, it is the lyre of Orpheus, it makes everything move, everything feel, everything attract. It renders the stones eloquent.

If we stand alone in front of a forest scene by Rousseau, as he was alone in his lean-to when he painted it, then we discover that the only meaningful heritage of Barbizon art lies in the paintings themselves. Because we can see the colors and brushstrokes the artist used, we can feel his gestures as he laid them down on his canvas. If we study a painting with love, we can feel the artist beside us, moving his hands.

35 DAUBIGNY. *The Beach at Villerville.* 1875

Bibliography

DESPITE the outpouring of books on the Barbizon artists from about 1880 to 1910, there are few which retain for us today anything beyond anecdotal interest. The following list includes all those which provide essential documentation, and those which are of value for the insights and historical judgments of their authors.

BAZALGETTE, LÉON. "Constable et les paysagistes de 1830," in his translation of C. R. LESLIE, John Constable, Paris, 1905.

BOUVIER, EMILE. La Bataille Réaliste, 1844–1857. Paris, 1914.

CANAT, RENÉ. Le Sentiment de la Solitude Chez les Romantiques et les Parnassiens. Paris, 1904.

Critics. The writings of the following critics spanning the years 1830 to 1875, for the most part gathered in anthologies: About, Astruc, Baudelaire, Blanc, Burty, Castagnary, Champfleury, Chesneau, Clarétie, DuCamp, Gautier, Pelloquet, Planche, Silvestre and Thoré-Bürger.

DORBEC, PROSPER. L'Art du Paysage en France. Paris, 1925.

HENRIET, FRÉDÉRIC. Le Paysagiste aux Champs. Paris, 1876.

MICHEL, EMILE. La Forêt de Fontainebleau dans la Nature . . . et dans l'Art. Paris, 1909.

MOLLET, JOHN W. The Painters of Barbizon. London and New York, 1890.

ROSENTHAL, LÉON. Du Romantisme au Réalisme . . . 1830–1848. Paris, 1914.

SAUVAGEOT, DAVID. Le Réalisme et le Naturalisme dans la Littérature et dans l'Art. Paris, 1889.

SLOANE, JOSEPH C. French Painting between The Past and The Present. Princeton, 1951.

TABARANT, ADOLPHE. La Vie Artistique au Temps de Baudelaire. Paris, 1942.

Corot

BAZIN, GERMAIN. Corot, revised edition. Paris, 1951.

DELTEIL, LOŸS. Le Peintre-Graveur Illustré, V. Paris, 1910.

DUMESNIL, HENRI. Corot, Souvenirs Intimes. Paris, 1875.

MOREAU-NÉLATON, ETIENNE. Corot Raconté par Lui-Même. 2 vols. Paris, 1924.

ROBAUT, A. and MOREAU-NÉLATON, E. L'Oeuvre de Corot. 4 vols. Paris, 1905.

SCHOELLER, A. and DIÉTERLE, J. Corot, Supplément à 'l'Oeuvre' . . . par A. Robaut . . . 2 vols. Paris, 1948 and 1958.

Daubigny

BOURGÈS, LÉONIDE. Daubigny, Souvenirs et Croquis. Paris, 1900.

DELTEIL, LOŸS. Le Peintre-Graveur Illustré, XIII. Paris, 1921.

HENRIET, FRÉDÉRIC. Charles Daubigny et son Oeuvre Gravé. Paris, 1875.

LARAN, JEAN. Daubigny. Paris, n.d. [1913].

Moreau-Nélaton, Etienne. Daubigny Raconté par Lui-Même. Paris, 1925.

Diaz

Bénézit, E. C. "Diaz," in Dictionnaire . . . des Peintres, Sculpteurs . . ., III, Paris, 1950.

Burty, Philippe. Maîtres et Petits Maîtres. Paris, 1877.

Clarétie, Jules. Diaz, catalogue of the retrospective exhibition, Paris, Ecole des Beaux-Arts, 1877.

Hédiard, Germain. Les Maîtres de la Lithographie. Paris, 1890–99.

Silvestre, Théophile. Histoire des Artistes Vivants. Paris, 1856; and Les Artistes Français. Paris, 1878.

Dupré

Bénézit, E. C. "Dupré," in Dictionnaire . . . des Peintres, Sculpteurs . . ., III, Paris, 1950.

Clarétie, Jules. Peintres et Sculpteurs Contemporains. Paris, 1873; and "M. Jules Dupré . . .," in series Les Hommes du Jour, Paris, 1878.

Delteil, Loÿs. Le Peintre-Graveur Illustré, I. Paris, 1906.

Hédiard, Germain. Les Maîtres de la Lithographie. Paris, 1890–99.

Hustin, A. "Jules Dupré," in l'Art. 47, 1889, pp. 155–64.

Mantz, Paul. Atelier Jules Dupré, catalogue of the sale at George Petit, Paris, January 30, 1890.

Jacque

Clarétie, Jules. Peintres et Sculpteurs Contemporains, 2ème série. Paris, 1884.

Guiffrey, J. L'Oeuvre [graphic work only] de Charles Jacque. Paris, 1866; Supplément. Paris, 1884.

Wickenden, Robert. "Charles Jacque," in Print Collector's Quarterly, I, 1912, pp. 71–101.

Millet

Bénédite, Léonce. The Drawings of J. F. Millet. London and Philadelphia, 1906.

Cartwright, Julia. See below "Sensier."

Delteil, Loÿs. Le Peintre-Graveur Illustré, I. Paris, 1906.

Gsell, Paul. Millet. London, 1928.

Moreau-Nélaton, Etienne. Millet Raconté par Lui-Même. 3 vols. Paris, 1921.

Naegeley [i.e., Gaëlyn], Henry. J. F. Millet and Rustic Art. London, 1898.

Sensier, Alfred [edited by P. Mantz]. La Vie et l'Oeuvre de Jean-François Millet. Paris, 1881. English edition, Boston, 1880 [sic]. The monograph by Julia Cartwright [Mrs. Helen Ady] of 1896, the only extensive monograph in English, is regrettably little more than a transliteration of Sensier. Many of Sensier's omissions and distortions were corrected by Moreau-Nélaton.

SOUILLIÉ, LOUIS. Les Grandes Peintres aux Ventes Publiques, Jean-François Millet. Paris, 1900.

Rousseau

BURTY, PHILIPPE. Maîtres et Petits Maîtres. Paris, 1877.

DELTEIL, LOŸS. Le Peintre-Graveur Illustré, I. Paris, 1906.

DORBEC, PROSPER. Théodore Rousseau. Paris, 1910.

GENSEL, W. Millet und Rousseau. Bielefeld and Leipzig, 1902.

SENSIER, ALFRED. Souvenirs sur Th. Rousseau. Paris, 1872; and Etudes et Croquis de Th. Rousseau, Reproduits et Publiés par Amand-Durand. Paris, 1873.

Troyon

DUMESNIL, HENRI. Troyon, Souvenirs Intimes. Paris, 1888.

GENSEL, W. Corot und Troyon. Bielefeld and Leipzig, 1906.

HUSTIN, A. Constant Troyon. Paris, 1893.

SOULLIÉ, LOUIS. Les Grandes Peintres aux Ventes Publiques, Constant Troyon. Paris, 1900.

Chronology

1791

Salon: L. Bruaudet exhibits *View taken in the Forest of Fontainebleau*; Georges Michel exhibits landscapes in the Salon from this year to 1814.

1796

July 17: Birth of Corot.

1797

Chateaubriand's "Letters on the art of drawing Landscape."

1803

Birth of Paul Huet.

1808

August 20: Birth of Diaz.

1810

August 28: Birth of Troyon.

1811

April 5: Birth of Dupré.

1812

Salon: Michallon exhibits *View of Saint-Cloud* and *Wash-house, study from nature*.

April 15: Birth of Rousseau.

1813

May 23: Birth of Jacque.

1814

October 4: Birth of Millet.

1816

Delacroix meets Bonington.

1817

First Prix de Rome for landscape established by the Academy.

February 15: Birth of Daubigny.

1819

Birth of Courbet.

1821

Colony of artists already established at Fontainebleau forest.

1822

Delacroix exhibits *Dante* in the Salon.

Corot begins painting full-time; studies with Michallon, then with J. V. Bertin; paints in Fontainebleau, Normandy and environs of Paris from 1822–25.

1823

Delacroix admires a Constable painting in Paris; shares studio with the British artist Thales Fielding.

Diaz and Dupré work together in a porcelain manufactory.

1824

Salon: Delacroix and Ingres rise to fame; Constable, Bonington and other British artists cause stir in Salon.

Birth of Monticelli.

1825

Birth of Boudin.

Corot to Italy.

1826

Corot in Italy.

Rousseau at studio of Rémond.

1827

Salon: Corot (first appearance).

Dupré working in porcelain manufactory in the Limousin; draws from nature.

Corot in Italy.

Rousseau painting in Fontainebleau.

1828

Corot returns from Italy.

Rousseau at studio of Guillon Lethière; paints in Fontainebleau.

1829

Corot in Normandy, Brittany and Fontainebleau.

Jacque working for engraver of maps.

1830

July Revolution in Paris; birth of Pissarro; Hugo's "Hernani."

Corot at Chartres, the Channel coast and elsewhere.

Dupré shows two landscapes in charity exhibition in Paris; paints in the Limoges district as well as near Paris.

Jacque begins six years' military service; publishes album of lithographs of military life; draws rural scenes in Burgundy.

Rousseau in the Auvergne; Ary Scheffer discovers him upon his return to Paris.

1831

Delacroix, Delaroche, Devéria, Decamps and others signal prominence of Romantic school; Hugo's "Notre-Dame of Paris"; Stendhal's "Red and Black."

Salon: Corot (first Fontainebleau subject), and Barye, Diaz, Dupré, Rousseau (first appearances).

Corot in Burgundy, Auvergne, Morvan, Fontainebleau.

Rousseau paints along the Seine and the Channel coast in Normandy.

1832

Birth of Manet.

Corot much at Fontainebleau.

Dupré painting in Berry.

Rousseau in Normandy and Brittany.

1833

Balzac's "Eugénie Grandet."

Salon: Corot (2nd class medal), Dupré (2nd class medal), Rousseau and Troyon (first appearance).

Corot at Rouen, Soissons, Normandy.

Dupré spends summer in Berry.

Jacque and Rousseau meet in Paris.

Millet goes to Cherbourg to begin professional training.

Rousseau and Dupré receive wide notice in the press; the Duc d'Orléans buys a Rousseau

painting; Rousseau spends summer in Saint-Cloud; allied with Daumier, Préault, Borel, Thoré and other Republicans; winter in Fontainebleau, his first long campaign there.

Troyon continues to decorate porcelain at Sèvres; paints in the neighborhood of Sèvres through the 1830's.

1834

Birth of Degas; Balzac's "Père Goriot"; Dumas' "Three Musketeers."

Salon: Corot, Diaz, Dupré, Rousseau (3rd class medal).

Corot's second trip to Italy.

Dupré in the Limousin; receives praise of Delacroix; visits England.

Millet studying in Cherbourg.

Rousseau meets Dupré; autumn in the Jura near Mont Blanc; begins to use bitumen under Ary Scheffer's guidance.

1835

82 museums now open in France (two in 1776); Gautier's "Mademoiselle de Maupin."

Salon: Corot, Diaz, Dupré, Rousseau, Troyon.

Corot paints in Fontainebleau.

Daubigny at Versailles painting decorations.

Dupré publishes in "l'Artiste" first of many lithographs.

Millet studies in Cherbourg.

Rousseau sells two sketches to the Prince de Joinville.

Troyon paints along the river Creuse.

1836

Salon: Corot, Diaz, Dupré, Rousseau, Troyon.

Corot in the Auvergne, at Avignon and Montpellier.

Daubigny spends most of year in Italy.

Dupré collaborates with Lami in painting battle scenes for Versailles.

Jacque goes to England where he does woodcut illustrations for Shakespeare editions.

Millet still at Cherbourg.

Rousseau's *Descent of the Cattle* rejected by

the Salon, exhibited by Scheffer in his studio; fall and early winter at Barbizon.

1837

Berlioz' "Requiem."

Salon: Corot, Diaz (first Fontainebleau subject), Troyon.

Daubigny restoring paintings in the Louvre.

Diaz meets Rousseau in Fontainebleau, is much taken by him.

Millet comes to Paris and enters studio of Paul Delaroche.

Rousseau exhibits at Nantes; goes to the Vendée where he begins *Valley of Tiffauge* and *Avenue of Chestnut Trees*; is commissioned to paint the Chateau de Broglie for the minister Guizot; at Barbizon in the fall.

Troyon paints in the Sologne.

1838

Opening of the Spanish Gallery in the Louvre.

Salon: Corot, Daubigny (first appearance), Diaz.

Corot sells two paintings to the Duc d'Orléans; at Orléans and Compiègne.

Daubigny begins to publish woodcut illustrations; collaborates with Meissonier in etching.

Jacque returns from England; begins to publish more book and magazine illustrations.

Millet works on his own in Paris.

Rousseau's *Avenue of Chestnut Trees* rejected by the Salon; exhibited in his studio where it is admired by Delacroix and George Sand; at Barbizon.

Troyon paints in Brittany.

1839

Birth of Cézanne.

Salon: Corot, Dupré, Troyon.

Corot at Rosny and Royat.

Daubigny spends autumn in the French Alps.

Rousseau at Barbizon.

Troyon exhibits a painting at Amiens; travels in Brittany.

1840

Birth of Monet.

Salon: Corot, Daubigny, Diaz, Millet (first appearance), Troyon (2nd class medal).

Corot has painting bought by the government; critics more favorably disposed; summer at Rosny and in the Morvan.

Daubigny spends six months in studio of Paul Delaroche; considerable success in providing magazine and book illustrations, his principal work for the next decade.

Dupré, Rousseau, Delacroix, Barye and others continue to plan for an artists' group to rival the Salon, but nothing results.

Millet spends the winter in Cherbourg.

Rousseau at Barbizon.

1841

Birth of Renoir.

Salon: Corot, Daubigny (exhibits etchings for first time), Diaz.

Corot in the Morvan.

Dupré and Rousseau share summer quarters at Monsoult, near l'Isle-Adam.

Millet returns to Cherbourg in autumn; paints many portraits.

1842

Musée Standish (many Spanish paintings) opened in the Louvre; Chevreul's course in the contrast of colors advertised at the Salon.

Salon: Corot.

Corot to the Jura and Switzerland, and to Mantes; the government buys one of his paintings.

Millet's entries rejected by the Salon.

Rousseau's first long campaign in Berry.

1843

By now about 400 periodicals being published in France (45 in 1812)

Salon: Corot, Daubigny.

Corot's *Destruction of Sodom* rejected by the Salon; his third trip to Italy.

77

Daubigny's first major painting campaign in Fontainebleau.

Dupré and Rousseau have adjacent studios in Paris.

Jacque publishes caricatures in "Charivari" 1843–44.

Troyon meets Rousseau and Dupré, goes with latter to the Landes; begins painting at Fontainebleau.

1844

Balzac's "The Peasants"; Boudin meets several of the Barbizon artists; Courbet's *Courbet au chien noir* in the Salon.

Salon: Corot, Daubigny (first Fontainebleau subject), Diaz, Millet, Troyon (first Fontainebleau subject).

Millet leaves Paris for Cherbourg.

Rousseau and Dupré go together to the Landes for five months.

1845

Salon: Corot, Daubigny (etchings only), Diaz, Jacque (etching only; first appearance).

Corot in Brittany and Normandy.

Daubigny spends summer at Valmondois.

Millet goes from Cherbourg to Le Havre, still painting portraits; paints seaside genre scenes; holds sale in Le Havre to finance his return to Paris in December.

Rousseau and Dupré share a studio at l'Isle-Adam in the autumn and early winter.

1846

Berlioz' "Damnation of Faust"; George Sand's "La Mare au Diable"; Michelet's "Le Peuple"; Chardin given first major study which confirms his budding revival.

Salon: Corot (Legion of Honor), Diaz, Jacque, Troyon (1st class medal).

Corot in Normandy, Brittany, the Limousin and Fontainebleau; Baudelaire and Champfleury mark his growing reputation.

Daubigny at Valmondois for the summer; also travels to Picardie.

Millet's Salon entry rejected; befriended by Diaz and meets Troyon; begins to paint peasant subjects.

Rousseau at l'Isle-Adam in the spring; he and Dupré have adjacent studios in Paris in the fall.

1847

Couture's *Romans of the Decadence* the chief attraction of the Salon.

Salon: Corot, Daubigny, Diaz, Millet.

Corot begins graphic work; henceforth has a number of official commissions.

Daubigny in the Morvan.

Dupré, Delacroix, Barye, Rousseau, Daumier, Jacque and others found an association to fight the Salon; it fails again.

Millet meets Rousseau, Jacque, Daumier and Barye in Paris; wins first important notice at the Salon for his *Oedipus*.

Rousseau's *Valley of Tiffauge* exhibited in Dupré's studio; he visits George Sand in Berry; paints at Sèvres.

Troyon spends the year in Holland where he is much taken by Dutch animal painters.

1848

February revolution in Paris; Republic established; birth of Gauguin.

Salon: Corot (2nd class medal), Daubigny (2nd class medal), Diaz, Millet (*The Winnower*), Troyon.

June: Millet, Rousseau and Jacque conscripted to fight insurgents.

Republican government commissions works from Millet, Rousseau, Dupré and Daubigny; Millet, Diaz and Daumier unsuccessful competitors for a figure of the Republic.

Association des Artistes exhibition includes works by Corot, Dupré and Rousseau.

Rousseau to Barbizon after the June Days; by now has permanent studio there.

1849

Salon: Corot, Daubigny, Daumier (first appearance), Millet, Rousseau (1st class medal; appears for first time since 1836), Troyon (Legion of Honor).

Corot exhibits in the Salon a plein-air painting for the first time (*The Colisseum*); in Douai and Normandy.

Daubigny in the region of Lyon; probably his first paintings of Optevoz.

Diaz auctions 80 paintings with poor results.

Dupré named to the Legion of Honor.

Millet and Jacque move to Barbizon in June.

1850

Courbet's *Burial at Ornans* creates a scandal in the Salon; Champfleury revives the Le Nain brothers.

Salon (December 1850–January 1851): Corot, Daubigny, Diaz (Legion of Honor), Jacque (3rd class medal for graphic art), Millet (*The Sower*), Rousseau, Troyon (first major animal picture).

Daubigny again at Optevoz and the Isère district.

Dupré retires to l'Isle-Adam.

Millet's *Sower* brings him notoriety.

Rousseau auctions 53 paintings with poor results.

1851

Boudin in Paris, shows influence of Troyon.

Corot travels extensively, including La Rochelle and Arras.

Daubigny paints along the Seine.

Diaz' fortunes improve with an auction of his works.

Millet exhibits a painting in London; begins to sell his drawings.

1852

Napoleon III constitutes the Second Empire.

Salon: Corot, Daubigny, Dupré, Rousseau (Legion of Honor).

Corot exhibits for the first time a plein-air painting of a French site *Port de la Rochelle*.

Daubigny meets Corot; they are together in Switzerland and in the Isère; Daubigny painting bought by the government.

Millet given a government commission, the

last breath of the Republican spirit for many years.

Rousseau instrumental in ending devastation of Fontainebleau forest by prompting government action.

Troyon in Normandy, begins there a remarkable series of animal pictures which include most of his famous works.

1853

Birth of Van Gogh.

Salon: Corot, Daubigny (1st class medal), Millet, Rousseau.

Corot at Fontainebleau, on the Channel coast, and elsewhere.

Daubigny meets Corot again in Switzerland; they paint together a folding screen; Napoleon III buys Daubigny's *Pond of Gylieu*.

Millet's three Salon paintings bought by M. Brimmer and W. M. Hunt, both of Boston; Hunt and W. Babcock, another American, seek out Millet in Barbizon and become his students; they and Rousseau are witnesses at his tardy marriage.

Troyon visits England.

1854

Corot goes briefly to the Lowlands.

Daubigny's first summer at Villerville, on the Channel coast near Trouville; early fall again in the Isère.

Jacque breaks with Millet and soon leaves the Barbizon group.

Millet spends the summer in the Cherbourg area.

Troyon begins his annual visits to his friend Loisel in Touraine, where he paints hunting dogs as well as other animals.

1855

All Barbizon artists except Dupré represented in Universal Exhibition in Paris, Rousseau and Decamps given special room and Corot, Rousseau and Troyon win first class medals; Courbet holds one-man exhibition; Pissarro and Whistler arrive in Paris; Pissarro visits Corot.

Daubigny, Diaz, Barye, Millet, Rousseau and Ziem plan together to illustrate an edition of La Fontaine's fables, but it proves abortive.

Daubigny summers in Normandy and Brittany.

Millet's first etching, with the help of Bracquemond.

1856

Corot in Normandy.

Daubigny travels to Rennes, Auxerre and the Morvan.

1857

Flaubert's "Madame Bovary."

Salon: Corot, Daubigny (Legion of Honor), Millet (*The Gleaners*), Rousseau.

Corot and Daubigny together at Auvers.

Daubigny exhibits in the Salon an etching after Ruysdael commissioned by the government; he is singled out by critics for his "impressions" of nature; he launches his studio-boat "le Botin" on the Oise river.

Rousseau's prices begin to fall after several years of prosperity; he goes to Picardie where he begins the *Village of Becquigny*; he has as informal students Charles Tillot, Emile Diaz and, with Millet's collaboration, also the daughter of their friend Laure.

1858

Monet meets Boudin; Thoré-Bürger begins revival of Vermeer.

Daubigny summers at Villerville; Corot visits him at Auvers.

1859

Birth of Seurat; Monet comes to Paris.

Salon: Corot, Daubigny, Diaz, Millet, Rousseau, Troyon.

Corot again at Fontainebleau.

Millet's *Angelus* completed; his *Death and the Woodcutter* rejected by the Salon, but exhibited in Paris and defended by Alexandre Dumas in an article; he exhibits two paintings in Marseille.

Troyon exhibits at Manchester and The Hague.

1860

Pissarro meets several of the Barbizon artists.

Most of the Barbizon artists join in an exhibition on the Boulevard des Italiens organized by L. Martinet.

Corot, Barye, Daumier, Millet, Rousseau, Troyon and Ziem form in Barbizon a Société Indépendante to rival the Salon; it atrophies.

Daubigny settles permanently at Auvers; Corot visits him.

Millet and Rousseau go briefly to Switzerland and Besançon; they greet in Barbizon the returned exile Thoré-Bürger.

Troyon exhibits at Brussels, Lyon, Bordeaux and Besançon.

1861

Boudin works with Troyon; Berthe Morisot works with Corot.

Salon: Corot, Daubigny, Jacque, Millet, Rousseau.

Corot in Fontainebleau.

Rousseau exhibits two paintings in Antwerp.

Troyon exhibits in Antwerp, Brussels and Bordeaux.

1862

Monet works with Jongkind.

Most of Barbizon artists continue to exhibit at Martinet's periodic exhibitions in Paris, as well as in Petit's exhibition of the Cercle de l'Union Artistique.

Corot spends a week in London.

Rousseau exhibits a painting in Brussels; discovers Japanese prints and begins to repaint his *Village of Becquigny* under their influence.

Troyon exhibits in London.

1863

Delacroix dies, Millet and Diaz at his funeral; Millet buys many Delacroix drawings at the posthumous sale; birth of Signac; Salon des Réfusés in which Manet and Whistler are prominent; Monet, Renoir, Sisley and Bazille paint in Fontainebleau; Berthe Morisot meets Daubigny.

Salon: Corot, Daubigny, Jacque, Millet (*Man with a Hoe*), Rousseau.

Millet begins collecting Japanese prints.

Rousseau holds another auction with poor results; in October goes to the Jura near Mont Blanc.

1864

Birth of Toulouse-Lautrec; Renoir meets Diaz in Fontainebleau; Pissarro exhibits in Salon as "pupil of Corot."

Salon: Corot (*Souvenir de Mortefontaine*), Daubigny, Jacque, Millet (1st class medal), Rousseau.

Millet's financial troubles by now over.

1865

Monet paints *Déjeuner sur l'herbe* in Fontaine-bleau; Renor and Sisley also paint there.

Salon: Corot, Daubigny.

Most of Barbizon artists exhibit with the Cercle de l'Union Artistique.

Corot, Dupré, Rousseau and Fromentin commissioned to paint the Demidoff town house.

Millet begins his large pastels.

Rousseau spends the spring on the Channel coast near Boulogne; large dealers' purchases restore his finances.

Troyon dies March 20.

1866

Salon: Corot, Daubigny, Millet, Rousseau.

Daubigny visits England, paints along the Thames; exhibits a painting in the Royal Academy; begins consistent defense of the Impressionists in the Salon.

Millet goes to Vichy and Clermont-Ferrand in early summer.

Rousseau called to court of Napoleon III for a visit.

Troyon given a retrospective exhibition in Paris.

1867

Universal Exhibition includes all Barbizon artists, Rousseau the head of the international jury; Courbet and Manet have one-man shows in Paris; Renoir paints *Lise* in Fontainebleau; exhibition at Barbizon includes Corot.

Daubigny summers in Brittany.

Jacque given Legion of Honor.

Millet spends the last half of the year caring for the dying Rousseau, after an early summer trip to Vichy.

Rousseau has large exhibition, mostly oil studies, which he helped organize; he dies on December 22.

1868

Salon: Corot, Daubigny.

Corot and Daumier decorate Daubigny's house at Auvers.

Dupré spends summer on Channel coast; begins period of many seascapes.

Millet receives several paintings of Rousseau which he is to finish for the collector Hartmann, whom he visits in the fall; to Vichy in early summer and to Switzerland in the fall; awarded the Legion of Honor.

1869

Salon: Corot, Daubigny.

Corot travels less frequently.

Daubigny spends ten days in Spain; he and Corot exhibit at the Royal Academy in London.

1870

July, war with Prussia; September, surrender at Sedan, Republic declared.

Salon: Corot, Daubigny, Millet.

Corot and Daubigny aid unsuccessful efforts to liberalize Salon rules.

Millet goes to Cherbourg during the war, Dupré to the Channel coast, and Daubigny to Villerville; in October Daubigny goes to London where he aids Monet; Pissarro also in London.

1871

January, France capitulates; March to May, the Commune in Paris, Courbet president of the Federation of Artists in which Millet refuses proferred membership.

Daubigny returns to Auvers in May; in September to Holland.

Millet in Cherbourg area until his return to Barbizon in November; some of his paintings sent to London by Durand-Ruel.

1872

Salon: Corot, Daubigny.

Corot buys house for Daumier in Auvers.

Daubigny goes to Cauterets in the Pyrenees, then to Villerville; buys a painting by Monet and meets Cézanne.

Durand-Ruel exhibits many paintings by Millet in Paris.

1873

Cézanne living in Auvers.

Salon: Corot, Daubigny.

Corot apparently works in Fontainebleau for the last time.

1874

First Impressionist exhibition.

Salon: Corot, Daubigny.

Corot finds Daubigny's *Les Champs au mois de Juin* too free and highly-colored.

Millet commissioned to paint a chapel of the Pantheon; he is unable to carry it out.

1875

Salon: Corot.
Millet dies January 20.
Corot dies February 22, after giving 10,000 francs to Millet's widow.

1876

Salon: Daubigny.
Daubigny travels along the Channel coast.
Diaz dies November 18.

1877

Salon: Daubigny.
Daubigny's last trip on his studio-boat.

1878

Daubigny dies February 19.
Durand-Ruel exhibits over 300 paintings of Barbizon school.

1887

The only major one-man show of Millet's work is held in Paris.

1889

Dupré dies October 6; the Barye Monument Society holds in New York the last major Barbizon exhibition until 1962.

1894

Jacque dies May 7.

COROT

JEAN-BAPTISTE-CAMILLE COROT (1796–1875). Corot was born in Paris on July 17, 1796. His parents were successful clothing merchants and Corot had a life of relative ease in contrast to the struggles of Millet or Rousseau. In 1822 he won over his parents and turned to painting full time, studying with the classicizing landscape painters Michallon and J. V. Bertin. He worked out-of-doors in Fontainebleau, the environs of Paris and along the Channel coast until he went to Italy in 1825. There he absorbed the classical tradition of landscape which he was never to forsake, while at the same time painting his spendid views of Rome and the Italian countryside with a clarity and directness that alone would have ensured his importance for later artists. Upon his return to Paris in the fall of 1828 (from Italy he had sent two pictures to the Salon of 1827), Corot established the rhythm of work which he and most other landscapists of the mid-century were to follow: during warm weather he painted out-of-doors, travelling throughout France, but in the winter months he prepared indoors his large paintings for the Salons. Four of his oils (including a Fontainebleau subject) appeared in the Salon of 1831, and he exhibited regularly thereafter. He won his first official recognition (a second-class medal) in 1833, but he was only slowly accepted as an artist of talent, and stirred none of the fierce winds that already raged around the person of Théodore Rousseau. In 1834 Corot went to Italy for the second time, remaining for about six months. The next year was the first in which he passed most of the warm season in Fontainebleau. The government bought his *Little Shepherd* (Metz Museum) in 1840, encouraging the critics to pay him more attention. Other government purchases and independent commissions followed and, by 1846, when he was decorated with the Legion of Honor, he was greeted on all sides as a major talent, although it was not until about 1860 that his works commanded high prices.

After six months in Italy in 1843, Corot travelled seldom outside France (brief trips to Holland in 1854 and London in 1862). He continued to range widely over his native country, but spent most of each year in the environs of Paris, especially at the family property in Ville d'Avray. By about 1850 he had grouped around him a number of disciples, including Chintreuil and Français and, though he did not offer formal training, he gave birth to an ever-widening group of landscape artists. He knew Rousseau, Millet, Troyon, Diaz and Dupré by the late 1840's, and met them often in Fontainebleau after the mid-century. He was also a friend of Barye and Daumier, both of whom frequented Fontainebleau, but of the whole group it was Daubigny with whom he established the closest friendship. They began painting together in 1852 and throughout their lives they exchanged visits as well as travelling in each other's company.

Corot exhibited an out-of-doors study for the first time in 1849 (*The Colisseum at Rome* [Louvre]), and his first plein-air painting of a French site in 1852 (*Port de la Rochelle* [Yale University Art Gallery]). For the public, his reputation rested upon his large studio compositions he exhibited in the Salons but, despite the prominence of his misty, Claudesque landscapes and his growing preoccupation with figure studies after 1855, his impact on younger artists came from his paintings done freshly from nature. By the mid-1860's his occasional contact with the young Impressionists fortified his significance for them, and ever since artist and layman alike have preferred Corot's unpretentious paintings from nature to his studio compositions. On February 22, 1875, just one month after Millet's death, Corot died in Paris.

10   COROT.   *The Forest of Fontainebleau.* 1846

1

The Inn at Montigny-les-Cormeilles.
c.1825–31
Oil on paper backed by canvas, 9¾ × 13
(24.7 × 33)
Collection: J. B. Neumann
Lent by the Jewett Arts Center, Wellesley
College
*The interlocked planes of this picture have often
been likened to the work of Cézanne and the
Cubists.*

2

The Old Beech Tree. c. 1828–30
Oil on canvas, 21⅞ × 18⅛ (55.5 × 46)
Signed lower right: *Corot*
Robaut no. 216
Collections: James Inglis; H. C. Angell
Lent by the Museum of Fine Arts, Boston

3

Farm at Recouvrières (Nièvre). 1831
Oil on canvas, 18½ × 27½ (47 × 70)
Signed and dated lower right: *Corot 1831*
(scratched into paint), *Corot* (painted over
initial signature)
Robaut no. 292
Collections: Pons; Diot, 1895; H. C. Angell
Lent by the Museum of Fine Arts, Boston
*Painted in the Nièvre, in central France, and
given by Corot to his host, Pons. Recent
cleaning has revealed "Corot 1831" scratched
into the paint underneath a later signature.*

4

Silenus. 1838
Oil on canvas, 97½ × 70⅞ (250 × 180)
Signed and dated lower right: *C. Corot 1838*
Robaut no. 368
Collections: J. Dollfus
Lent by Mr. Jerome Hill
*Exhibited in the Salon of 1838, and typical of
the pictures by which Corot was known in the
thirties. Its figures look to Poussin and the
landscape, to Claude.*

5

Woman Seated with Sickle. 1838
Oil on canvas, 10¾ × 26 (27 × 66)
Signed and dated lower left: *C. Corot 1838*
Robaut no. 380

Collections: Léon Meinard; Alfred Robaut;
P.-A. Chéramy; Philippe de Saint-Albin;
Albert S. Henraux
Lent by Mr. William A. Coolidge, Topsfield,
Mass.
*A curious picture reflecting not the study of
French rural life, but the Italianate figures
that in the hands of artists like Léopold Robert
laid the groundwork for later paintings of the
French peasantry.*

6

Grove with Seated Woman. c. 1840
Pen and pencil on paper, 15⅜ × 10³⁄₁₆
(39 × 25.9)
Stamped lower left: *Vente Corot*
Robaut no. 2719
Collections: Corot Sale, 1875; Alfred
Robaut, 1880
Lent by the Musée des Beaux-Arts, Lille

7

The Church at Lormes. c. 1841
Oil on canvas, 13½ × 18¼ (34.2 × 46.4)
Signed lower right: *Corot* over an earlier
signature
Robaut no. 423
Collections: Fromanger Benefit Sale, 1874;
Anonymous Sale, 1877; R. E. Dietrich, 1927;
Lord Ashfield, 1950
Lent by the Wadsworth Atheneum
*The delicate, matte tone of each hue results
from Corot's habitual mixing of white with
his colors.*

8

Landscape with Cattle. c. 1842
Oil on canvas, 16⅜ × 29¾ (41.5 × 75.5)
Signed lower left: *Corot*
Robaut no. 510
Collections: Berthelier, 1889; James J. Hill;
Louis W. Hill
Lent by Mrs. Hannes Schroll, San Francisco

9

The Destruction of Sodom. 1843,
reworked 1857
Oil on canvas, 36⅜ × 71⅜ (92 × 181)
Signed lower right: *Corot*
Robaut nos. 460 and 1097
Collections: Durand-Ruel, 1873; Comte
Abram de Camondo, 1889;

Mrs. H. O. Havemeyer, 1929
Lent by the Metropolitan Museum of Art

*This very Romantic painting, exhibited in the
Salon of 1857, is a much-altered version of a
composition rejected by the Salon of 1843, but
accepted the following year. For the 1857
exhibition, Corot cut the canvas considerably at
the top and the right, and reworked the entire
surface so that relatively little remains of the
original composition. Such a painting strikes
us today as unusual because we have in mind
the fresh paintings of nature which dominate
our image of Corot. The latter are closest to
Impressionism while paintings like "Sodom,"
which harmonize with the more Romantic
works of Daubigny and Rousseau, show how
much a part of his own generation Corot was.*

10

The Forest of Fontainebleau. 1846
Oil on canvas, 35⅝ × 51 (90.5 × 129.5)
Signed lower left: *Corot*
Robaut no. 502
Collections: Alfred Robaut, 1872; S. M. Vose;
Beriah Wall; S. D. Warren
Lent by the Museum of Fine Arts, Boston

*Based in part on a study of 1834, and exhibited
in the Salon of 1846. It seems to reflect an
awareness of Rousseau, with whose Auvergne
painting of 1837 (No. 90) it should be compared
to demonstrate their common roots in the
Dutch tradition.*

11

Village Street, Dardagny. 1853
Oil on canvas, 13½ × 9½ (34 × 24)
Signed lower left: *Corot*
Robaut no. 718
Collections: Louis Fréret, 1873; Albert
Wolff, 1875; Th. Bascle; Collis P. Huntington
Lent by the Metropolitan Museum of Art

*Probably painted in 1853, when Corot was
with Daubigny in the Swiss village of
Dardagny. They had been there together the
previous year for a shorter visit which began
their close friendship.*

12

Mother Protecting her Child. c. 1855–58
Oil on canvas, 19⅞ × 14⅛ (50.5 × 36)
Signed lower left: *Corot*

Robaut no. 1264
Collections: Gustave Greux; John D.
McIlhenny
Lent by the Philadelphia Museum of Art

*Two trees on the left were painted over by
Corot later, but the composition was never
terminated. The motif is common in Millet's
earlier work, and both artists often painted
mothers with children in the decade of the fifties.*

13

Village near Beauvais. c. 1855–65
Oil on canvas, 15¾ × 11⅞ (40 × 30)
Signed lower right: *Corot*
Robaut no. 1003
Collections: Verdier; Clapisson, 1885;
Thomy-Thiéry, 1902
Lent by the Musée du Louvre

14

Night Landscape. c. 1859–73, unfinished
Oil on canvas, 47⅜ × 39 (121 × 99)
Signed lower left: *Corot*
Lent by the Johnson Collection

*An unfinished painting which raises problems
that might be solved by its inclusion in a large
Corot exhibition. Aside from the signature,
probably added after Corot's death, the liquid
style and the subject both are similar to compositions like Dante and Virgil (versions of
1859 and 1873), Macbeth (1859), and
Don Quixote (1868). The last (Cincinnati
Art Museum) was apparently done with the
aid of Daubigny's son Karl, and gives rise to
the possibility that this painting might be a
similar collaborative effort.*

15

*The Sèvres Road (Sèvres-Brimborion, vue
prise en regardant Paris).* c. 1864
Oil on canvas, 18¼ × 24 (46.3 × 61)
Signed lower right: *Corot*
Robaut no. 1463
Lent by the Lucas Collection, on permanent
loan to the Baltimore Museum of Art

*Richard Lucas of Philadelphia was the means
of bringing many Barbizon pictures to this
country. He visited the artists themselves, and
bought this painting directly from Corot about
1865. A nearly identical variant is in the
Louvre.*

1

16

Souvenir de Mortefontaine. 1864
Oil on canvas, 25⅝ × 35 (65 × 89)
Signed lower right: *Corot*
Robaut no. 1625
Collections: Napoleon III
Lent by the Musée du Louvre

*One of Corot's most famous paintings from
the time of its exhibition in the Salon of 1864.
It is the finest of several variants which, with
their studies, comprise a veritable cycle. The
"souvenir" of the title echoes the nostalgia for
an arcadian past which was so prominent a
part of nineteenth-century poetry and
painting.*

17

Girl with a Pink Shawl. 1865–70
Oil on canvas, 26¼ × 21¾ (67 × 55)
Stamped lower left: *Vente Corot*
Robaut no. 1580
Collections: Corot Sale, 1875, no. 474; Vérane;
H. C. Angell
Lent by the Museum of Fine Arts, Boston

18

*La Bacchanale à la source; Souvenir de
Marly-le-Roi.* c. 1872
Oil on canvas, 32½ × 26 (82.5 × 66)

Signed lower left: *Corot*
Robaut no. 330
Collections: Émile Gavet; Brun; Marquis
Fressinet de Bellanger; H. S. Henry;
Mr. and Mrs. Robert Dawson Evans; the
Misses Abby and Belle Hunt
Lent by the Museum of Fine Arts, Boston

*Unrivalled for the variety of its colors within
the delicate harmony of the whole.*

19

Coast at Étretat. 1872
Oil on canvas, 14 × 22½ (35.5 × 57.1)
Signed lower left: *Corot*
Robaut no. 2054
Collections: Oscar Simon, 1894; Isaac Cook;
Warner S. McCall
Lent by the City Art Museum of St. Louis

*With its relatively flat tones, closer to the late
seaport paintings of Troyon and Dupré than
to those of Daubigny.*

20

Landscape. c. 1860–68
Black crayon, 9⅞ × 15 (25.2 × 38.1)
Signed lower left: *Corot*
Collections: Quincy Adams Shaw
Lent by the Brooklyn Museum

2

4

5

12

6

8

11

9

3

20

13

14

15

16

CROT

19

17 COROT. *Girl with a Pink Shawl.* 1865–70

DAUBIGNY

CHARLES DAUBIGNY (1817–78). Daubigny was born in Paris on February 15, 1817. It was natural for a boy whose father was a landscape painter, and whose family included several other artists, to begin drawing and painting in early youth. Cast on his own at an early age, Daubigny studied assiduously, managing a six-month's trip to Italy in 1836, in between jobs as a painter of ornaments and restorer. In 1838, with the help of his friend Meissonier, he began to publish woodcut illustrations. Few paintings survive from the next decade, when his chief activity was innumerable book and magazine illustrations, and independent etchings of landscape. From 1838 he began to exhibit landscapes regularly in the salon, both oils and etchings. For six months in 1840 he studied with Paul Delaroche, who was also Millet's teacher. His first major painting campaign in the forest of Fontainebleau was in 1843, but he remained throughout his life more faithful to Valmondois and Auvers, where he had spent his youth.

In 1848 Daubigny won his first Salon prize, a second-class medal, and the following year the Republican government commissioned from him an etching after Claude Lorrain. This, and the publication of two albums of etchings in 1850 and 1851, cemented his reputation as a graphic artist. As a painter he only gradually came to prominence after 1850. The government bought a view of the Seine (Nantes Museum) in 1852, followed by a first-class medal and Louis Napoleon's purchase of his *Pond of Gylieu* (Cincinnati) the next year. From the time of his first important contact with Corot in the summer of 1852, Daubigny gave ever greater place to his landscapes painted directly from nature, his preferred sites being the regions of Optevoz, southeast of Lyon, the Oise, just north of Paris, and Villerville, on the Channel coast. To facilitate his plein-air painting, Daubigny launched his "Botin" in 1857, a studio-boat in which he travelled up and down French rivers until his death.

By about 1858, already accepted as a major landscape artist, Daubigny began to raise critical disputes for his directness and his lack of traditional finish. In the next decade, often accused of rendering only the "impression" of nature, he opened the way for Impressionism perhaps more than any other painter. His direct heirs were modest artists like his son Karl, and he continued to produce studio landscapes, but younger artists like Monet and Pissarro found in his fresh paintings of nature the inspiration for more radical innovations.

The Universal Exhibition of 1867 consecrated Daubigny's reputation, despite the critical arguments surrounding his paintings from nature, and he found a ready market for his work. While remaining faithful to his chosen regions around Paris and along the Channel, he travelled to London in 1866 and again in 1870–71, during the war and the Commune. During his second stay in London he aided Monet, like himself an exile, and in 1872 he bought one of the younger artist's paintings of Holland (they had both been in Holland in 1871). This, and his first meeting with Cézanne near Auvers in 1872, symbolize the increasing significance of his art for the coming generation. Daubigny died on February 19, 1878.

30   DAUBIGNY.   *Landscape near Pontoise.* 1866

21

The Harvest. 1851
Oil on canvas, 53⅛ × 77⅛ (135 × 196)
Signed lower left: *Daubigny 1851*
Lent by the Musée du Louvre

*Exhibited in the Salon of 1852, and acquired
by the state in the following year. While its
freshness is uniquely Daubigny's, the broad
fields and prominent sky recall Dutch
seventeenth-century landscape, as does the
considerable distance between our imaginary
position and the foreground of the painting.*

22

The Mill at Optevoz. 1852–57
Oil on canvas, 34⅛ × 59 (86.7 × 149.8)
Signed lower right: *C. Daubigny 1857*
Collections: William L. Elkins
Lent by the Philadelphia Museum of Art

*The site is Gobelle's mill at Optevoz and was
painted several times by the artist (the best-
known version is in the Metropolitan Museum).
This studio painting was based on studies
dating from 1852, and has the heavy brushwork of Courbet which made a strong
impression on Daubigny from 1852.*

23

*The Pond of Gylieu (L'Etang de Gylieu
près Optevoz).* 1853
Oil on canvas, 24½ × 39¼ (62.2 × 99.7)
Signed lower left: *Daubigny*
Collections: Napoleon III; M. de Rainbeaux
père; M. de Rainbeaux fils, 1925; Mr. and
Mrs. John Hauck; Mrs. Emilie L. Heine
Lent by the Cincinnati Art Museum

*This painting, bought by Napoleon III, was
the artist's first major triumph and was
universally admired in the Salon of 1853. The
site is near Optevoz, one of Daubigny's
favorite spots just south of Lyons, where he
had painted in the summer of 1852 in the
company of Corot. Daubigny himself made a
woodcut of the composition for* L'Illustration.

24

Old Woman Seated by an Oil Lamp. c. 1854
Charcoal on buff paper, 9¹⁵⁄₁₆ × 15¼
(25.2 × 38.7)
Note on verso: "*Bought May 2nd 1891 in*

*Auvers-sur-Oise, S et O, from Mme Veuve
Karl Daubigny by S. E. C. Oliver*"
Collections: S. E. C. Oliver; Lee M. Friedman
Lent by the Museum of Fine Arts, Boston

25

Coast near Villerville. 1855
Oil on canvas, 21½ × 45⅝ (54.5 × 115.9)
Signed and dated lower right: *Daubigny 1855*
Collections: W. G. Mather
Lent by the Cleveland Museum of Art

*During his first summer at Villerville (on the
Channel near Trouville) in 1854, Daubigny
was struck by the vast grandeur of the seacoast,
embodied in his panoramic composition. Later
he preferred lighter, more intimate views
which are less overtly Romantic in feeling.*

26

Sunset on the Seine. 1856
Oil on canvas, 19¼ × 35½ (49 × 90)
Signed and dated lower right: *Daubigny 1856*
Collections: Walter Richmond, 1899;
H. C. Angell
Lent by the Museum of Fine Arts, Boston

*The dark and liquid palette date from well
before 1869, the traditional reading of the
indistinct date next to the signature. Upon
close examination, only the final digit remains
in doubt, and it seems to be "6." Known works
in this style are spread over the years 1850–60
when, despite the general lightening of his
palette, Daubigny's latent Romanticism still
was in evidence in sunsets and moonlit scenes.
The dimensions were reduced when the
painting was altered in the early 20th century.*

27

River Scene near Bonnières. 1857
Oil on panel, 11¾ × 21⅛ (29.8 × 53.6)
Signed and dated lower left: *Daubigny 1857*
Collections: Henry K. S. Williams
Lent by the California Palace of the Legion
of Honor

*The village of Bonnières on the Seine near
Mantes was the subject of several paintings
including the Salon picture of 1861 (Edinburgh)
which is a variant of this composition. Here
his contact with Corot has helped overcome the
heavier palette of the early fifties.*

28

Women Washing along the Oise (Les Laveuses, effet de soleil couchant sur l'Oise). 1859
Oil on canvas, 17 × 35½ (43 × 90)
Signed lower right: *Daubigny 1859*
Collections: Alfred Chauchard, 1906
Lent by the Musée du Louvre

Perhaps the Salon painting of 1859, whose catalogue description is too general to make it certain.

29

Le Hameau au bord d'un ruisseau. 1865
Crayon and charcoal, 12¾ × 22¼ (32.5 × 56.5)
Signed lower right: *Daubigny 1865*
Collections: Beurdeley
Lent by the Musée du Louvre

30

Landscape near Pontoise. 1866
Oil on canvas, 44⅛ × 63⅝ (112 × 161.5)
Signed and dated lower left: *Daubigny 1866*
Collections: Parmentier
Lent by the Kunsthalle, Bremen

Not only was this site frequented by Pissarro and others, but the style also shows how much the Impressionists were indebted to Daubigny.

31

Les Dunes. c. 1871
Oil on canvas, 21¾ × 25¾ (55.2 × 65.3)
Signed lower left: *Daubigny*
Collections: Hendrik Willem Mesdag, 1920
Lent by Col. T. A. H. Coltman

32

The Mills of Dordrecht. 1872
Oil on canvas, 33½ × 57½ (85 × 146)
Signed lower left: *Daubigny 1872*
Collections: Yerkes, 1910; James Warren Lane, 1924; Mr. and Mrs. E. Raymond Field, 1932
Lent by the Detroit Institute of Arts

Daubigny spent about two weeks in Holland in 1871, and in a letter of September 14, he writes of sketching the mills in Dordrecht. The sketches were later worked into final paintings in Paris, and this one was in the Salon of 1872. Van Goyen and van de Velde come to mind,

but Cuyp's seascapes are even closer, especially his painting of the same title at Kenwood, in London.

33

The Mountain Stream, Cauterets. 1873
Oil on canvas, 32¼ × 46⅞ (82 × 119)
Signed lower right: *Daubigny*
Collection: Daubigny Sale, 1878, no. 294
Lent by the Stichting Willem van der Vorm

Daubigny went to Cauterets in the Pyrenees for an asthma cure in the summer of 1872. Although he complained that (unlike Rousseau) he found it impossible to realize in painting the grandeur of the mountains, this splendid composition is certainly of the Pyrenees. The discreet intensity of the painting is less dramatic than Rousseau or Baroque mountain scenes but, for that reason, more effective to modern eyes. It resembles Ruysdael's Mountain Waterfall *which Daubigny must have seen when he visited the National Gallery in London the previous year.*

34

Fields in June. 1874
Oil on canvas, 53 × 88 (134.6 × 223.6)
Signed lower left: *Daubigny 1874*
Collection: Mr. and Mrs. Louis V. Keeler
Lent by the Andrew Dickson White Museum of Art, Cornell University

Exhibited in the Salon of 1874, this painting's tapestry of bright color and free brushwork raised again the objections of many observers (including Corot) who found it too "impressionistic." A comparison with the Harvest of 1851 *(No. 21) shows how Daubigny has brought the foreground forward on the surface.*

35

The Beach at Villerville. 1875
Oil on panel, 15 × 25¾ (38 × 65.4)
Signed lower right: *Daubigny 1875*
Collections: Daubigny Sale, 1878, no. 334; Alexander Young, 1910; Miss L. Coats
Lent by Mr. John Tillotson

One of the most enchanting of Daubigny's late paintings. It is essentially a variant of the Salon painting of 1864 (Mesdag Museum) but more free in every respect.

36
Landscape. c. 1877
Oil on canvas, 25⅛ × 18⅞ (64 × 48)
Signed lower left: *Daubigny*
Collections: Mrs. A. B. Blodgett;
Mrs. Martin T. Fiske Collord
Lent by the Metropolitan Museum of Art

*The composition harks back to those of the early
fifties, but has the crisp directness and humid
greens of Daubigny's late Auvers palette.*

21

22

24

26

25

27

28

29

33

32

34

36

DIAZ

Virgile Narcisse Diaz de la Peña (1808–76). Diaz was born of Spanish emigrant parents in Bordeaux on August 20, 1808. Although he was orphaned in early youth and lost a leg in an accident while still a boy, Diaz' life and art are the incarnation of a bubbling, charming spirit. Like Renoir and so many artists of the nineteenth century, he began as a porcelain painter (he and Dupré worked in the same porcelain manufactory in 1823), and a short stay with the painter Souchon comprised all his formal training. His most typical work of the 1830's and 1840's reflects the taste of the group of young Romantics around Gautier and Borel: oriental women, Spanish bathers, or nymphs. He admired Delacroix, whose style continued to be an inspiration throughout his life, but he was even more caught up in the Romantic love of the naughty vignette and the *scène galante*, a rebirth of the eighteenth century French tradition. His early landscapes, though often done from nature, were also in a rather light Rococo vein, but from his first Salon (1831) he consistently exhibited landscapes in which the impact of Rousseau became more evident. He met Rousseau in the Fontainebleau forest in 1837, which was also the year in which he exhibited in the Salon his first Fontainebleau subject. He knew Corot, Troyon, Jacque, Dupré and Millet by 1847, and thereafter met them often in Fontainebleau; in the winter his Paris studio often served as a meeting place for the others.

Diaz was recognized as a soul-mate by Gautier and his friends in the mid-1830's, and by the middle of the century his sheer brilliance and charm had won him a wide set of admirers and a life of comfort, even if his type of painting could never find official approval. He continued to paint gypsies and nymphs for the rest of his life, delightful paintings which remind us of Delacroix, Decamps and Correggio, and which had a decisive influence on Monticelli. But most younger artists were drawn to his landscapes. He exhibited rarely after the mid-century (his last Salon was in 1859), but they could usually find him in Fontainebleau, Paris and its environs since he seldom travelled farther afield. Renoir, Sisley, Pissarro and Monet all passed under his spell in the 1860's. His tapestry-like canvases of undergrowth speckled with sunlight were a link with the decorative tradition of the eighteenth century, and provided surfaces of rich and varied lights which they found congenial. Diaz died at Menton on November 18, 1876.

37

The Courtesans. c. 1835–40
Oil on panel, 11½ × 17¾ (29 × 45)
Signed lower left: *N. Diaz*
Collections: Thomas Wigglesworth; Mrs. W.
Scott Fitz; Edward J. Holmes
Lent by the Museum of Fine Arts, Boston

*Although Diaz did similar subjects all his life,
the relative separation of lights and darks, and
the uniform treatment of foliage, point to an
early date. The face of the young woman
furthest to the right looks like Bonington's ladies,
for the artist went through a Bonington phase
in the late thirties. The whole invokes Diaz'
heritage: Correggio, the eighteenth century,
Prud'hon, and Delacroix.*

38

*Descent of the Bohemians (Bohémiens se
rendant à une fête).* 1844
Oil on canvas, 39 × 31½ (99 × 80)
Signed lower left: *N. Diaz*
Collections: Paul Périer, 1846; M. A. M.,
1849; Getting; Mme. Ernest André; Mrs.
S. D. Warren.
Lent by the Museum of Fine Arts, Boston

*The variety of tone and texture of this painting,
exhibited in the Salon of 1844, shows the fruits
of Diaz' close study of nature since the time
he met Rousseau in 1837. The figures are of
the same family as Decamp's and Delacroix'
oriental subjects, but the delicate juxtaposition of
a wide choice of hues in the large light patch
near the center will later be found in Courbet.*

39

Flowers. c. 1845–50
Oil on canvas, 14⅝ × 11½ (37.5 × 29)
Signed lower right: *Diaz*
Collection: Jacob Stern
Lent by the California Palace of the
Legion of Honor

*Diaz had painted flower pieces during the
thirties, but in a Rococo manner which gave
way to this more robust style in the following
decade.*

40

Common with Stormy Sunset. 1850
Oil on panel, 14⅝ × 21½ (37 × 54.5)

Signed and dated lower left: *N. Diaz 50*
Collections: Alexander Young, 1886;
George Salting, 1907
Lent by the National Gallery, London

41

The Forest of Fontainebleau. 1858
Oil on panel, 19⅞ × 29 (50.5 × 73.5)
Signed and dated lower left: *N. Diaz 58*
Collection: Arthur J. Secor
Lent by the Toledo Museum of Art

42

Wood Interior. c. 1867
Oil on canvas, 22 × 41½ (56 × 104)
Signed lower right: *N. Diaz*
Collection: Charles P. Parsons
Lent by Washington University

*This and the Toledo painting of 1858 are
superb examples of Diaz' unique style. He was
an ally of Rousseau, whose forest interiors are
generally similar, but Diaz' almost phosphorescent flecks of pigment move over the
surface to produce a rich texture that has for us
today the attraction of Monet's late work and
even of Abstract Expressionism.*

43

Landscape. c. 1870–75
Oil on panel, 16¾ × 21½ (42.5 × 54.6)
Stamped lower right: *Vente Diaz*
Collection: Diaz Sale, 1877
Lent by Mr. Anthony Bampfylde

*This unfinished study exposes the structure of
such paintings as the* Valley Marsh *(No. 44),
whose lightness and grace result from the
intial patchwork of transparent strokes.*

44

Valley Marsh. 1872
Oil on canvas, 23 × 29 (58 × 73.5)
Signed and dated lower right: *N. Diaz 72*
Collection: Mrs. Emilie L. Heine
Lent by the Cincinnati Art Museum

45

Landscape with Figures
Watercolor, 9⅞ × 13¼ (25 × 33.6)
Damaged and restored in the sky
Signed lower left: *N. Diaz*
Lent by the Kunsthalle, Hamburg

37

43

39

41

44

45

40

DUPRE

JULES DUPRÉ (1811–89). Dupré was born in Nantes on April 5, 1811. His father was a porcelain manufacturer and the young Dupré was already an apprentice in the trade in 1823 when he met Diaz. His only formal training was a brief period with the landscape and animal painter Diébolt. Like Rousseau, Dupré drew and painted directly from nature at an early age. His first dated works are from 1827, when he was attached to his father's business in the Limousin. He exhibited three landscapes in 1831, his first Salon, and soon became a friend of Rousseau and Troyon. In 1833 he won a second-class medal and was noticed by the press as a painter who dared paint freshly from nature. The impact of seventeenth century Dutch painting was visible in his works by 1822 and, after a brief journey to England the following year, an awareness of Constable was also apparent. From 1835 to 1840 his name was often bracketed with that of Rousseau; he had a wide circle of friends, including Decamps and Lami, and seemed likely to win a major place in French art.

One of the great enigmas of the Barbizon school is the subsequent position of Dupré. Reversing the usual evolution, he became progressively more "Romantic" after 1835, more concerned with generalized landscape, and he gradually forsook direct study from nature as the nucleus of his art. Until their falling-out in 1849, he was intimately associated with Rousseau; they travelled extensively together and shared quarters. But in 1850, after having been decorated with the Legion of Honor, Dupré suddenly withdrew to l'Isle-Adam north of Paris, and spent the rest of his life in virtual retirement. In 1852 he appeared in the Salon for the first time since 1839, but his only major exhibition after that was the Universal Exhibition of 1867. From the late 1860's he frequented the Channel coast more and more, and his finest late works are his seascapes. He came out of his self-imposed retirement in 1876 and lived for several years in Paris, but he seems to have ceased all important activity by about 1880. He died on October 6, 1889, at l'Isle-Adam, about fifty years after the period of his greatest importance for French landscape painting. It is nonetheless certain that throughout the middle third of the century, his paintings, though infrequently exhibited, provided singular lessons in the virtues of carefully wrought skies and a dense impasto which embodied the materiality of natural forms.

46

Plateau de Belle-Croix. 1830
Oil on canvas, 68 × 58 (172.7 × 147.3)
Signed and dated lower right: *Jules Dupré 30*
Collections: Arthur Stevens;
Mrs. Mary N. Emery
Lent by the Cincinnati Art Museum

*A remarkable painting which shows why
Dupré was so important in the thirties.
Rousseau later gave him credit for teaching
him how to construct a composition, and here in
1830 we see why, for Dupré has already a
consummate sense of pictorial organization.*

47

Landscape with Oak Grove. 1833
Black crayon with touches of blue and
red-orange wash on buff paper
17¾ × 24½ (45 × 62.2)
Signed and dated lower right: *Jules
Dupré 1833*
Collection: Alfred Sensier
Lent by Mr. John Goelet

48

The Duck Pond (La Vanne). c. 1845–48
Oil on canvas, 20⅛ × 27⅛ (51 × 69)
Signed lower left: *Jules Dupré*
Collections: Wertheimber, 1861; Emile Gavet;
Van Praet, 1892; Alfred Chauchard, 1906
Lent by the Musée du Louvre

*No better painting exists to show the mutual
exchanges which resulted from the intimate
friendship of Dupré and Rousseau, both of
whom frequently used this tight, almost dotted
brushwork. In both subject and technique it
looks forward to such Impressionist paintings
as Renoir's Duck Pond of 1873 (Louvre).*

49

On the Road. 1856
Oil on panel, 15½ × 20 (39.3 × 50.8)
Signed and dated lower right: *Jules
Dupré 1856*
Collections: Thomas N. Page;
Henry Field, 1894.
Lent by the Art Institute of Chicago

*One of Dupré's favorite compositions which
exists in several variants, including those in the
Louvre and in the Wadsworth Atheneum,*

*Hartford. Their chief variation is in the
skies, on which Dupré lavished special
attention.*

50

Cottage by the Sea. c. 1865–70
Oil on panel, 8½ × 18⅛ (21.5 × 46)
Signed lower left: *Jules Dupré*
Collections: Durand-Ruel, 1893; H. C. Angell
Lent by the Museum of Fine Arts, Boston

51

The Headland (Point de Dunes). c. 1870–75
Oil on canvas, 28½ × 36 (72.5 × 91.4)
Signed lower left: *Jules Dupré*
Collection: James Donald
Lent by the Glasgow Art Gallery
and Museum

*Dupré's late work is largely devoted to sea-
scapes, whose echoes of Holland fortify their
Romantic mood.*

52

Fishing Boat on the Beach. c. 1880
Oil on canvas, 29 × 36½ (73.6 × 92.7)
Signed lower right: *Jules Dupré*
Collection: J. Bell
Lent by the Collection of
Mr. Walter P. Chrysler, Jr.

53

Landscape with Brook
Charcoal on paper, 16⅜ × 11⅞ (41.6 × 30.1)
Signed lower left: *Jules Dupré*
Collection: Louis V. Black
Lent by the Fogg Art Museum,
Harvard University

47

49

51

52

53

JACQUE

CHARLES-EMILE JACQUE (1813–94). Jacque was born on May 23, 1813, in Paris. After a brief apprenticeship with an engraver of maps, he spent the years 1830 to 1836 in military service, during which he visited the Lowlands. He published lithographs of military life and drew rural scenes in Burgundy, where he was stationed for a time. From 1836 to 1838 he was in London, where he continued his career as a graphic artist with illustrations for Shakespeare. Upon his return to Paris he embarked on a career that paralleled Daubigny's, doing a great many illustrations for various books and magazines, including some caricatures for "Charivari." He first exhibited an etching in the Salon of 1845, and won a third-class medal for graphic arts in the Salon of 1850–51.

Until about 1850 his work, nearly exclusively prints and drawings, shows a strong influence of seventeenth century Dutch art. In 1849 he had moved to Barbizon with Millet, and from then on was under the sway of the stronger artist. Jacque was for several years a close friend of Millet and Rousseau, but his ungenerous temperament led to a rupture with the other Barbizon artists in 1854, and he left the village. He shortly found some success in painting as well as in prints, and for the rest of his life he lived comfortably in the environs of Paris, where he could keep an eye on his several experiments in animal husbandry. In 1861 he was given official notice as a painter, winning a third-class medal. A more vigorous style from that time on helped make him a popular artist with many patrons in the Lowlands, the British Isles, and the United States. Jacque died in Paris on May 7, 1894. In restrospect his reputation seems to us today to have rested upon his reflection of more significant talents, particularly Millet and Troyon, but his drawings and prints rescue him from mediocrity and can be studied with great pleasure.

54

Behind the Farmhouse. 1846
Pencil on paper, 4¾ × 8½ (12 × 21.5)
Signed upper left: *Ch. Jacque 1846*
Lent by Mr. and Mrs. S. Van Berg

55

Tree with Sheep. c. 1850–55
Charcoal and crayon, heightened with white,
on gray paper, 20⅞ × 16½ (53 × 42)
Signed lower right: *Ch. Jacque*
Collections: Jacque Sale, 1894, no. 78;
Mrs. Jeanette L. Windegger
Lent by the City Art Museum of St. Louis

56

The Old Forest. c. 1855–70
Oil on canvas, 32⁷⁄₁₆ × 26⅜ (83 × 67)
Signed lower left: *Ch. Jacque*
Collection: Mrs. William A. Putnam
Lent by the Brooklyn Museum

57

Sheep Leaving a Farmyard. 1860
Oil on panel, 22 × 28½ (56 × 72)
Signed upper left: *Ch. Jacque 1860*
Collection: Borie, 1886
Lent by the Johnson Collection

*Although Jacque is strongest as a draftsman
and printmaker, he turned ever more to
painting after 1850, and these two oils have a
frankness that rewards patient observation.*

54

55

56

57

MILLET

JEAN-FRANÇOIS MILLET (1814–75). Millet was born in the village of Gruchy, near Cherbourg, on October 4, 1814. His parents, Norman peasants, acknowledged his early inclination to art, and the young Millet had his first professional training in Cherbourg from 1833 to 1836, with the painters Mouchel and Langlois. A fellowship awarded by the city of Cherbourg took him to Paris in 1837, where he studied for a time with Paul Delaroche. He had a portrait accepted in the Salon of 1840, but no longer any regular source of income, and for the next decade suffered the rigours of severe want. From 1841 to 1845 he divided his time between Paris and the cities of Cherbourg and Le Havre, doing a great many portraits as well as paintings and pastels in a manner close to Diaz. About 1846 he began to paint in a stronger manner, continuing with sculptural nudes and *scènes galantes*, but also turning to seaside and rural genre. By 1847 he was on friendly terms with Diaz, Rousseau, Jacque, Daumier, Barye, Dupré and Troyon. His *Oedipus Taken Down from the Tree* (Ottawa), exhibited in the Salon that year, was the first work to draw widespread comment. Gautier, among others, praised him highly while looking askance at his free and heavy brushwork.

1848 was the year in which Millet's fortunes took a decided turn for the better. His *Winnower* (later destroyed) suited the new Republican spirit and was admired in progressive circles; it was purchased by the Republican minister Ledru-Rollin. In the winter of 1848–49, the government commissioned *Haymakers Resting* (Louvre), and the money permitted Millet, Jacque and their families to move to Barbizon in June, 1849. Although the immediate reason was to escape the cholera and political upheavals of Paris, it is evident that Millet had been moving rapidly toward peasant subjects in preceding years. Once in Barbizon he embraced wholeheartedly the rural environment and thenceforth non-rural subjects had a minor place in his art.

Shortly after *The Sower* (Philadelphia) brought him notoriety in the Salon of 1850–51, Millet began to make a modest living by selling his superb drawings and, occasionally, some paintings. In the 1850's his friendship with the Boston painter William Morris Hunt provided him with important American patrons, and he had modest success with Dutch collectors as well. In Barbizon Millet drew close to Rousseau after 1850, and for the rest of their lives they were the most intimate of friends. Rousseau had a studio in Barbizon, but returned to Paris for the winter months; Millet remained the year around in the Fontainebleau village until his death. His only important trips outside Barbizon were to the Cherbourg area in the summer of 1854, to Vichy and its environs in the summers from 1866 to 1868, and again to Cherbourg in 1870 to 1871. Most of his subjects were from Barbizon and, largely from memory, from his Norman homeland. He was, however, the most cultured artist of the mid-century next to Delacroix, and his familiarity with Virgil, Theocritus, La Fontaine and Milton is shown in his many drawings.

Accused of being a socialist in 1851, Millet continued to affront the middle class with paintings of rural life which, though fatalistic rather than revolutionary, asserted the moral superiority of hard labor. *The Gleaners* (Louvre) and the *Man with a Hoe* (Mrs. Henry Russell) in the Salons of 1857 and 1863, were his most controversial paintings.

After 1863, encouraged by his intimacy with Rousseau, Millet devoted himself to land-scape more often, and he gradually became more acceptable to the public. He was already well known abroad, but his financial troubles only came to an end in 1864, when he won a first-class medal. About 1865 he began what many regard his greatest works—his large pastels. He had always used this medium, but from 1865 to 1869 he produced over a hundred pastels which combined his greatest gift, drawing, with a palette of high-toned color. These, together with his innumerable drawings and many oils, make him second only to Corot among the Barbizon artists for the diversity of subjects and types of composition.

The Legion of Honor was awarded Millet in 1868, and he grew progressively more famous. During the war and the Commune he stayed in Cherbourg, where he painted some of his most splendid seascapes. He was commissioned to decorate a chapel of the Pantheon in 1874, but he died at Barbizon on January 20, 1875, without being able to fulfill the government order. The irony of Millet's life and art is that he was virtually deified for his Biblical spirit, whereas in reality he was a life-long agnostic. In the last quarter of the century this erroneous belief resulted in the isolation of one part of his production, which in turn led to his being today the most misunderstood of the entire Barbizon school.

58

Comtesse de Valmont. c. 1841
Oil on canvas, 37⅞ × 31⅛ (96 × 79.5)
Signed lower right: *J. F. Millet*
Collections: Charles Heyman; Otto
Ackermann; Col. H. Bühler
Lent by the City Art Museum of St. Louis

*Painted about 1841 when Millet did a great
many portraits in both Cherbourg and Paris.
This painting appears to be a pendant to*
The Lawyer Valmont *of the same dimensions
and style (private collection, New York). They
are rather like the contemporary portraits of
Couture and other students of Paul Delaroche.*

59

The Quarriers. c. 1846
Oil on canvas, 29 × 23½ (74 × 60)
Signed lower right: *J. F. Millet*
Collections: Millet Sale, 1875, no. 3;
Ichabod T. Williams; Arthur J. Secor
Lent by the Toledo Museum of Art

The manière fleurie *identifies this as a
painting of about 1846, when extensive
quarrying was undertaken in Paris for the
new railroads. The Michelangelesque pose of
the upper figure is close to Daumier, with
whom Millet exchanged important stylistic
impulses.*

60

Reclining Nude. c. 1846
Black chalk on white paper, 6 × 11¼ (15 × 28.5)
Stamped lower right: *J. F. M.*
Collections: Henri Rouart; Ernest Rouart
Lent by Mme. Jacques Dupont

*Once owned by Henri Rouart, Degas' good
friend. Millet's many paintings and drawings
of nudes used to be viewed only as a means of
his earning money, but such superb drawings as
this prove him to be a great master of the
female form which dominates his art from
about 1844 to 1848.*

61

Mother and Child (Les Errants). 1846–50
Oil on canvas, 19½ × 15 (49.5 × 38)
Signed lower right: *J. F. Millet*
Collection: Horace Havemeyer
Lent by the Denver Art Museum

*Parallel to his paintings in a Rococo manner
stemming from Diaz, Millet developed a more
robust style, usually devoted to such Romantic
themes as distraught fishermen's families or
homeless wanderers. In both style and subject
they precede the paintings of Daumier on whom
they had a strong influence.*

62

The Lovers. c. 1846–50
Black chalk on tan paper, 12¾ × 8⅝ (32.4 × 22)
Stamped lower right: *J. F. M.*
Collections: James S. Inglis; Charles Deering
Lent by the Art Institute of Chicago

*Rousseau had a collection of Roman and
Renaissance coins and medallions, which may
have inspired this drawing. Millet was always a
sculptural draftsman, and this composition
has remarkable affinities with Rodin's famous
Kiss.*

63

The Sower. 1850
Oil on canvas, 42⅛ × 33⅞ (107 × 86)
Collections: Détrimont; A. Sensier; Harry
Payne Whitney, 1942
Lent by Mr. Julius H. Weitzner

*This unpublished canvas, once owned by
Millet's frame-maker and dealer Détrimont,
should be situated between the two versions of
his famous composition. He apparently found
the first version (Museum of Fine Arts, Boston)
too crowded and, late in 1850, began the second
(Provident Trust, Philadelphia). In a large
drawing and in this canvas, he altered the
drawing of the figure, lowering his outstretched
arm and shoulder, pulling in his leg, and
simplifying all the modelling. Most of the
elements of the figure were flattened onto the
surface at the same time. Millet often retained
the full-scale sketch, as in this case, and worked
out the final composition on another canvas,
which was sent to the Salon in December, 1850.*

64

Starry Night. c.1850–51
Oil on canvas mounted on wood,
23¾ × 32⅛ (65 × 81.5)
Signed lower right: *J. F. Millet*
Collections: Millet Sale, 1875, no. 32;
George Lillie Craik;
J. S. Knapp-Fischer
Lent by the Yale University Art Gallery

*Millet's closest friendship was established with
Rousseau, and apparently as a result he turned
increasingly to landscape after 1850. In the
winter of 1851–52 he wrote to Rousseau that
he preferred to all the excitement of Paris*

*such sights as "the little star sparkling in its
cloud, as we saw together one night after a
splendid sunset." The poignancy and somber
intensity of this painting have already
prompted observers to think of Van Gogh's
Starry Night. The painting was probably
retouched in the area around the trees about
1866–68.*

65

The Spinner. 1851–55
Oil on canvas, 18⅛ × 15⅜ (46 × 39)
Signed lower right: *J. F. Millet*
Collections: J. W. Wilson, 1874;
Quincy Adams Shaw
Lent by the Museum of Fine Arts, Boston

*A study of the painting on the reverse of a
drawing for The Harvesters of 1851–53
implies that it was begun in 1851. The smooth
surface is from Millet's style of 1855, when he
was preoccupied with interiors whose eloquent
simplicity echoes the work of Chardin and
the seventeenth-century Dutch.*

66

Woman Seated, with Cow. 1852
Black chalk, 16½ × 12¼ (41.8 × 31.2)
Signed and dated center right: *J. F. M. 1852*
Collections: Hermann Eisler; F. Koenigs
Lent by the Museum Boymans-van Beuningen

67

The Milkmaid. Begun 1854, unfinished
Oil on canvas, 21¾ × 18 (55.2 × 45.7)
Stamped lower right: *J. F. Millet*
Collections: Millet Sale, 1875, no. 15;
Sir George A. Drummond, 1919;
Mr. and Mrs. George Tweed
Lent by the Tweed Gallery, University of
Minnesota, and Mrs. Edward L. Tuohy

*The painting was first drawn on canvas in the
summer of 1854, which Millet spent in his
native region of Cherbourg, and was worked on
sporadically thereafter without ever being
finished.*

68

The Gleaners. c. 1856
Oil on canvas, 15 × 12 (38 × 30.5)
Signed lower right: *J. F. Millet*
Collections: Mrs. Henry Codman Potter;

Alfred Corning Clark; E. S. Clark
Lent by the Museum of Fine Arts,
Springfield, Mass.

*This and a nearly identical variant (Alfred
Daber) were probably completed before the
great* Gleaners *of 1857 (Louvre). Six major
drawings for this vertical composition suggest
that it was an autonomous painting, not just
a study for its famous successor.*

69

*Rabbits in the Gorges d'Apremont,
sunrise.* 1859–60
Oil on canvas, 19¾ × 24⅛ (50.1 × 61.3)
Signed lower right: *J. F. Millet*
Collection: Millet Sale, 1875, no. 21
Lent by Mr. Denys Sutton

*The handsome coloration of the rock alone
disproves the view that Millet was only a
draftsman insensitive to the qualities of paint.*

70

Man with a Hoe. 1859–62
Oil on canvas, 32 × 39½ (81 × 100)
Collections: E. Blanc; Alfred Stevens;
Prosper Crabbe; E. Secrétan; Defoer, 1886;
Van Den Eynde; Mr. and Mrs. William H.
Crocker
Lent by Mrs. Henry Potter Russell

*One of the most famous paintings in the history
of Western art, for many years erroneously
listed as having been destroyed in the San
Francisco fire of 1906. Millet wrote on July 21,
1860, that the painting was far along and in
another letter of December 29, 1862, he
announced its completion. It was the highlight
of the Salon of 1863. Defending himself against
the bitter attacks upon the painting, he wrote
on May 30, 1863: "There are those who tell me
that I deny the charms of the countryside. . . .
I see very well the haloes of the dandelions,
and the sun which, far across many lands,
stretches out its glory among the clouds. I see
no less . . . in a rocky spot, a man completely
exhausted, whose oofs! have been heard since
morning, and who tries to straighten up for a
moment to catch his breath." The beautifully
wrought terrain makes us realize that there is
more in the painting than the fatalistic image
of man.*

71

Meridian. c. 1865–68
Pastel on paper, 28⅜ × 38¼ (72 × 97.2)
Signed lower right: *J. F. Millet*
Collections: Emile Gavet; William L. Elkins
Lent by the Philadelphia Museum of Art

*In 1865 Millet began to devote himself to
pastels, which over the next five years became
his major output. Bruegel seems to have given
him the courage to create such monumental,
blocky forms. Together with the radical fore-
shortening, these chunky figures look forward
to Orozco and Picasso in our century.*

72

Twilight. c. 1866.
Crayon and pastel on paper, 20 × 15¼ (51 × 39)
Signed upper right: *J. F. Millet*
Collections: Emile Gavet; Quincy Adams Shaw
Lent by the Museum of Fine Arts, Boston

*Much like Seurat later, on whom he had a
profound influence, Millet liked twilight and
nocturnal scenes which let him exploit his
penchant for shadowy forms and the still
melancholy of tired beings and waning light.*

73

Hillside near Vichy. 1866
Ink on paper, 4¼ × 4½ (10.7 × 11.4)
Stamped lower left: *J. F. M.*
Collections: Millet Sale, 1875; Lucien Guiraud
Lent by M. César de Hauke

*Three variants in the Louvre expose the fact
that Millet's apparently casual drawings were
carefully constructed. The elegant simplicity
of the inked lines and the prominent use of
untouched paper are in contrast to the dense
compositions of a decade earlier, an evolution
traceable in part to Millet's passion for
Japanese prints which he had begun collecting
in great numbers by 1864.*

74

Farmyard in Winter. 1868
Pastel on paper, 26¾ × 34¾ (68 × 88)
Signed lower right: *J. F. Millet*
Collections: Emile Gavet; Quincy Adams Shaw
Lent by the Museum of Fine Arts, Boston

75

Primroses. 1868
Pastel on paper, 15¾ × 18⅞ (40 × 48)
Signed lower right: *J. F. Millet*
Collections: Emile Gavet, 1875; Quincy
Adams Shaw
Lent by the Museum of Fine Arts, Boston

76

The Buckwheat Harvest. 1868–74
Oil on canvas, 33½ × 43¾ (85 × 111)
Signed lower right: *J. F. Millet*
Collections: Frédéric Hartmann, 1881;
Quincy Adams Shaw
Lent by the Museum of Fine Arts, Boston

Summer *of the four seasons commissioned in
1868 by Rousseau's erstwhile patron, Hartmann. Although an August scene, an
autumnal air is suggested by the purple tones
which are faithful to the color of buckwheat.
The drawing of the two foreground figures is
the strongest indication of Millet's importance
for Van Gogh. Canvas for the painting was
ordered on April 17, 1868, and on March 18,
1874, Millet wrote that it needed only a final
stroke or two. Of the same series,* Autumn
is in the Metropolitan Museum, Winter *in the
National Gallery of Wales, and* Spring *in
the Louvre.*

77

The Shepherdess. 1869–71
Oil on canvas, 64 × 44¼ (162 × 130)
Signed lower right: *J. F. Millet*
Collections: Millet Sale, 1875, no. 35;
S. D. Warren
Lent by the Museum of Fine Arts, Boston

*In 1869 Millet posed his daughter Marguerite
in his studio, and only caught the pose he
wanted when she started at the sight of a mouse.
The painting retains in the opening hands and
alert head some of this feeling, especially when
compared with the known preliminary drawings, but Millet's instinctive grasp of the monumental has created an image of permanence.*

78

The Birdnesters. 1869–74
Oil on canvas, 29 × 36½ (73.5 × 93)
Signed lower right: *J. F. Millet*
Collections: Millet Sale, 1875, no. 53; Félix

Gérard, 1896; William L. Elkins
Lent by the Philadelphia Museum of Art

*Begun in 1869, this strange painting was the
last on which Millet worked before he died. It
represents the killing of pigeons in Normandy,
a nighttime sport in which the birds, stupefied
by the glare of torches, are knocked from
hedgerows. Despite their dynamic movements,
the figures have a curious quattrocento feeling,
bringing to mind Masaccio and Fra Angelico.*

79

The Sailboat. 1871
Oil on canvas, 9⅞ × 13 (25 × 33)
Signed lower right: *Millet*
Collection: Quincy Adams Shaw
Lent by the Museum of Fine Arts, Boston

*During the Franco-Prussian War and the
Commune, Millet was in Cherbourg where he
painted a number of superb seascapes. Here
the palette is close to that of Delacroix'
seascapes.*

80

The Church at Gréville. 1871–74
Oil on canvas, 23⅝ × 29 (60 × 73.5)
Signed lower left: *J. F. Millet*
Collection: Millet Sale, 1875, no. 50
Lent by the Musée du Louvre

*Begun in 1871 in his native village, the painting
was slowly completed over the next three years.
Its richly varied colors and thick surface
make it perhaps Millet's finest landscape. Even
the portions in shadow are rendered with a
kaleidoscope of hues, delicately interrelated.*

81

Pasture in Normandy. 1871–74
Oil on canvas, 29 × 36½ (73.6 × 92.7)
Signed lower left: *J. F. Millet*
Collections: J. de Kuyper, 1911; James J. Hill;
Mrs. Clara Hill Lindley
Lent by the Minneapolis Institute of Arts

*Long considered a painting of the Auvergne,
the site is without question the slopes of Normandy, near Cherbourg, whose topography,
trees, animals and peasant costume are all here
characterized. The high horizon line is typical
of Millet's late landscapes, which move
forward to the surface in contrast to the style
of the mid-century.*

77   MILLET.   *The Shepherdess.* 1869–71

58

60

62

61

65

66

67

68

69

73

71

72

74

75

76

78

80

81

79 MILLET. *The Sailboat.* 1871

ROUSSEAU

PIERRE-ETIENNE-THÉODORE ROUSSEAU (1812–67). Rousseau was born on April 15, 1812. His father and mother had a successful draper's business in Paris, and among their relatives were several artists, chief among them Théodore's cousin Alexandre Pau de Saint-Martin, a landscape painter. Rousseau began painting with his cousin at an early age and when only fourteen was already studying professionally with the painter Rémond. But more important were his copies after Claude and the Dutch masters and, above all, his early penchant for painting directly from nature. He made long painting excursions in the environs of Paris, including Fontainebleau, from 1826 to 1829. In 1830 he marked the end of all formal study (he had worked for a while with Guillon Lethière) by a lengthy stay in the Auvergne, where he painted astonishing studies from nature which have a Fauve-like liberty and intensity. Upon his return to Paris, his Byronic paintings attracted the noted painter Ary Scheffer, through whom Rousseau soon became known to progressive circles in Paris. He appeared regularly in the Salon from 1831 to 1836, and rapidly became the most controversial figure in landscape, occupying a position analogous to that of Delacroix. His works were purchased by the Duc d'Orléans, and championed by the young Romantics led by Gautier and Borel. By 1834 he had associated himself with Jacque, Dupré, Daumier, Préault, Thoré and others known for their radical politics. He was not a militant by nature, but he remained faithful to the Republican credo for the rest of his life.

During the 1830's Rousseau travelled extensively throughout France, preferring the rather savage sites of the Auvergne, the Jura, and the then primitive sections of Fontainebleau forest. Following the lead of his friend Dupré, he journeyed to more placid regions in the 1840's, especially to the Landes near Bordeaux and to Berry. The emotional canvases of the 1830's were now accompanied by more straightforward paintings of nature. He was excluded from the Salon from 1837 to 1847, and only with great difficulty managed to sell enough to live by, despite the friendship of Delacroix, George Sand, and others. He returned to the Salon in 1849 (he could have exhibited the previous year but had nothing ready) with three paintings in his more Romantic manner, and affirmed his reputation as the most important landscape painter of the July monarchy. He won a first-class medal from the liberal jury, enough to insure a rise to respectability which lasted several years.

Rousseau had always worked regularly in the forest of Fontainebleau, but about 1837 he began to rent a studio in Barbizon nearly every year, and soon settled there on a permanent basis. His friendship with Dupré, broken in 1849, was replaced by the closest association of his life, with Millet. He travelled less often after the mid-century (his only ventures outside France were to cross the border into Switzerland), partly because he had the care of an insane wife whom he refused to have committed. His winter quarters in Paris, and his summer studio in Barbizon, were the preferred gathering places for the Barbizon artists, for whom Rousseau was the guiding spirit. In 1867 he won singular honors in the Universal Exhibition, but they came too late. He died in Millet's arms on December 22, 1867, at the age of 55, the one man more than any other around whom the battle over landscape had been waged since 1830.

82

The Bridge at Moret. 1828–29
Oil on canvas, 10½ × 13¾ (26.6 × 35)
Signed lower left: *TH. R.*
Collections: Auguste Rousseau, 1900;
Vicomte de Turel, 1918
Lent by the Smith College Museum of Art

*This painting follows closely the description of
views of Moret dated 1828–29 in Rousseau's
1867 exhibition and, save for a discrepancy in
dimensions, might well be number 8 in that
catalogue.*

83

Country Road with Poplars (La Chasse).
1830–40
Charcoal on buff paper, 12³⁄₁₆ × 19¼ (31 × 49)
Lent by the Museum of Fine Arts, Boston

84

The Torrent. c. 1830
Oil on canvas, 14¾ × 18⅛ (37.5 × 46)
Signed lower left: *TH. Rousseau*
Collection: Auguste Rousseau, 1900
Lent by the Museo Nacional de Bellas Artes
de Buenos Aires

85

Cottages in Normandy. 1831
Oil on panel, 4⅞ × 13½ (12.3 × 34.2)
Signed lower left: *TH. R.*
Collections: Philippe Burty; E. Strauss
Lent by Mrs. John Woolf

*Another of the early pictures included in the
1867 exhibition, unusual at the time for the
freedom of its liquid brushwork.*

86

The Jetty at Granville. 1831
Oil on canvas, 6¹⁵⁄₁₆ × 16¹⁵⁄₁₆ (17.5 × 43)
Signed lower right: *Th. R.*
Collections: Baron Nathaniel de Rothschild;
Antony Roux, 1914; A. de Rothschild, 1950
Lent by the Wadsworth Atheneum

*One of the early paintings selected by Rousseau
himself for his exhibition in 1867. He and
Corot were both attracted often to this Norman
seaport. Rousseau's astonishing vigor at this
date, when he was only nineteen, is controlled
by the solidity of his pigments which seem to*

*embody the substance of the materials they
represent. In the back-lit boats to the left one
can see the beginnings of a motif which was to
become almost obsessive during the rest of the
century for hosts of landscape artists.*

87

La Plaine de Chailly. c. 1833
Oil on panel, 10½ × 13¼ (26.5 × 33.5)
Signed lower left: *TH. Rousseau*
Collections: Alexander Young, 1910;
W. McArthur, 1914; Dr. Crompton
Lent by Mr. John Tillotson

88

Descent of the Cattle. 1835
Oil on canvas, 102 × 65⅜ (258.8 × 166)
Lent by the Musée de Picardie, Amiens

*One of the great causes célèbres of nineteenth-
century art. In late 1834, when in the village
of Gex near Mont Blanc, Rousseau was struck
by the descent of the cattle to their winter
quarters, a procession which lasted two days.
Upon his return to Paris in December, he began
the painting in the studio of Ary Scheffer, upon
whose advice he used bitumen which has partly
ruined the picture. Rejected by the Salon jury
of 1836, it was exhibited in Scheffer's studio
that year and again in 1838. It was championed
by Scheffer, Delacroix and George Sand, and
its Byronic sublimity cemented the artist's
reputation as the leading landscape painter of
his generation. Because of inadequate
documentation, one can only guess that the
larger variant in the Mesdag Museum was the
final composition and this canvas, the major
preliminary version.*

89

*The Forest at Fontainebleau, Bas-Bréau
(Le Vieux Dormoir).* Begun winter 1836–37,
finished in 1867
Oil on canvas, 25½ × 40½ (65 × 103)
Signed lower left: *Th. Rousseau*
Collections: Laurent-Richard, 1873;
Charles Pillet, 1881
Lent by the Musée du Louvre

*Begun during the winter of 1836–37, and
finished years later for the Salon of 1867, this
painting was the result of a lifetime's work,*

*involving many drawings and oil studies. The
site is the "Dormitory" where cattle sought
the liquid coolness of the forest, and of which
Rousseau was especially fond. The dense
interlace of foliage is that side of Rousseau's
art which strongly attracted Diaz after they
became friends in 1837.*

90

In the Auvergne Mountains. 1837
Oil on canvas, 25½ × 31⅞ (64 × 81)
Signed and dated lower right: *Th. Rousseau
1837*
Collections: S. D. Warren; Arthur J. Secor
Lent by the Toledo Museum of Art

91

Valley of Tiffauge (Marais en Vendée).
1837–41
Oil on canvas, 25½ × 40½ (64.7 × 103)
Signed lower left: *Th. Rousseau*
Collections: Baroilhet; Papeleu, 1856;
Lt. Gen. Goethals; Laurent-Richard; Peyrot,
1881; H. Vever, 1897; E. Glaenzer; F. Ames;
C. T. Yerkes; Mr. and Mrs. John Hauck;
Mrs. Emilie L. Heine
Lent by the Cincinnati Art Museum

*Entitled by Rousseau the Marais en Vendée,
and given the derisive nicknames, The Muddle
and The Soup of Weeds, it is one the artist's
most important works. He demonstrates the
pictorial richness of the modest aspects of
nature heretofore deemed unworthy of a major
composition. It was worked on steadily until
about 1841, and was probably retouched in
1843 or 1844 when it was sold to the collector
Baroilhet.*

92

Lowland Marsh (Marais de la Souterraine).
1842
Oil on paper on canvas, 8¾ × 11½ (22 × 29)
Collection: Normand
Lent by Mr. John Tillotson

*One of Rousseau's most personal paintings, it
represents the submerged marshes of the Berry.*

93

Village in Berry. 1842
Oil on canvas, 13½ × 20½ (34.2 × 52)

Signed lower left: *Th. Rousseau*
Collections: H. N. Smith, 1872; F. W. Weld,
1886; Mrs. H. B. Duryea; Mr. and Mrs. John
Hauck; Mrs. Emilie L. Heine
Lent by the Cincinnati Art Museum

*The summer of 1842 spent in Berry is only
rivalled in the number of splendid paintings
by Rousseau's Auvergne campaign of 1830.
This painting calls to mind Hobbema and
A. van de Velde in both subject and composition.*

94

The Sandy Moor. c. 1842–44
Ink over black chalk on paper, 7⅞ × 11¼
(20 × 28.4)
Stamped lower right: *TH. R.*
Collections: Rousseau Sale, 1868, no. 347 or
no. 363; Alexander Reid
Lent by the National Gallery of Scotland

95

Under the Birches (Le Curé). 1842–44
Oil on panel, 16⅝ × 25⅜ (42 × 64.5)
Signed lower left: *Th. Rousseau*
Collections: Rousseau Sale, 1868; Dr. Véron;
Henri Didier; Baron Nathaniel de Rothschild;
Georges Gould; Arthur J. Secor
Lent by the Toledo Museum of Art

*The painting was begun at Le Fay in Berry
where Rousseau had gone following the urgings
of Dupré, who had long made of it a favored
site. A country priest rides along the sunken
path in the center (hence the nickname
Le Curé), wrapped against the cool autumn
evening whose moisture has thickened the
atmosphere. Such screens of trees, which tend
to flatten the composition, are often found in
Rousseau's work and will later be the basis for
Monet's series of poplar trees.*

96

*Le Givre (Uplands of Valmondois near
l'Isle-Adam).* Winter of 1844–45
Oil on canvas, 25 × 38⅝ (63.5 × 98)
Collections: Constant Troyon; Laurent-
Richard, 1878; Febvre; Baron E. de
Beurnonville, 1880; William T. Walters
Lent by the Walters Art Gallery

*During the winter of 1844–45, Dupré and
Rousseau shared quarters at l'Isle-Adam,
north of Paris. Rousseau set himself the task*

of painting the effects of frost on the slopes of
Valmondois and, like Monet later, did the
painting in a burst of concentrated effort that
lasted a week. The picture was executed
out-of-doors on a white canvas. Partial
restoration of a generation ago presents a
difficult problem: The misty tone of the middle
distance, partly stripped away, might have
been intentional, or might be the accidental
result of Rousseau's mixing fatty oils and
varnish with his pigments. Troyon owned the
picture and lent it to an exhibition in Antwerp
in 1861. It might also have been the Terrains
d'automne exhibited in the Salon of 1849.

97
Farm on the Banks of the Oise. 1852
Oil on canvas, 16⅛ × 25⅛ (41 × 64)
Signed and dated lower right:
TH. Rousseau 52
Collections: Vicomte D'Aquila; E. Bruggaman,
1882; W. H. Vanderbilt
Lent by Mr. George Howard

98
*Route dans la forêt de Fontainebleau,
effet d'orage.* c. 1860–65
Oil on canvas, 11¾ × 20⅛ (30 × 51)
Signed lower right: *Th. Rousseau*
Collection: Alfred Chauchard, 1906
Lent by the Musée du Louvre
*The dab-like brushstrokes and translucent
tones of many late works suggest that Rousseau
was not immune to the work of Diaz, but he*

had a more varied palette and a feeling for the
power of nature different from the charm that
typifies his friend's paintings.

99
The Oak Tree (Chêne de roche). c. 1861
Pencil on paper, 9⅛ × 11 (23 × 28)
Stamped lower right: *TH. R.*
Collections: Rousseau Sale, 1868, no. 337(?);
François Ehrmann père; François Ehrmann
fils
Lent by M. Jean Ehrmann

100
Sunset near Arbonne. c. 1865
Oil on panel, 25¼ × 39 (64 × 99)
Signed lower left: *TH. Rousseau*
Stamped lower right: *TH. R.*
Collections: Rousseau Sale, 1868; Robert
Graves, 1887; Collis P. Huntington
Lent by the Metropolitan Museum of Art
*One of the handsomest of the many heavily-
charged sunsets which Rousseau painted
throughout his life. The present surface of the
painting dates from about 1865, but it was
probably worked on over a period of many
years.*

101
La Lande aux genêts.
Black crayon with pastel, 23⅝ × 35⅜ (60 × 90)
Collection: Alfred Bruyas
Lent by the Musée Fabre, Montpellier

84

85

86

87

90

91

92

93

96

98

94

97

99

101

TROYON

CONSTANT TROYON (1810–65). Troyon was born on August 28, 1810, into a family of porcelain painters, and remained attached to the porcelain manufactory at Sèvres well after he began to exhibit paintings in the Salon. His first Salon paintings in 1833 and 1835 were landscapes of the Sèvres district, but gradually he moved further afield, especially in Brittany and the Limousin. In 1843 he met both Rousseau and Dupré, and went with the latter on a painting trip to the Landes. He also began frequenting the forest of Fontainebleau, which dominated his subjects of the next few years. He won a third-class medal in 1838, and a first-class honor in 1846, a token of his gradual acceptance as an artist whose work was never controversial, and whose placid temperament permeated his calm landscapes.

Troyon's trip to Holland in 1847 was the decisive event of his career, for he there fell under the sway of Dutch animal painting and for the rest of his life was known as an animal painter. His nomination to the Legion of Honor in 1849 guaranteed financial success, and he became the first Barbizon artist to win general acceptance. His works were exhibited abroad more often that those of any other artist of the group—London, Manchester, Brussels, Vienna, Antwerp and the Hague. By 1860 he had a more marked impact on artists outside France than any living French artist. In nearly every European capital he had a host of followers who made of animal painting one of the most pervasive offshoots of landscape. Troyon remains today the strongest painter of animals of the nineteenth century, perhaps because he was first a landscape painter and always provided an intimate dialectic between his animals and their natural environment. Although his major landscapes after 1848 are found in his animal pictures, he turned more frequently to seascapes in the late 1850's and, like Dupré and Millet, his finest pure landscapes of his last years are of the Channel coast.

Aside from brief trips to England and the Lowlands, Troyon spent most of his later years in Normandy, the Touraine, and the environs of Paris. He died on March 20, 1865, after a brief period of insanity the importance of which has usually been exaggerated.

106   TROYON.   *The Pointer* (Le Chien d'arrêt). 1860

102

Tobias and the Angel. 1841
Oil on canvas, 65⅜ × 94½ (166 × 240)
Signed lower left: *C. Troyon 1841*
Lent by the Wallraf-Richartz-Museum

*Exhibited in the Salon in 1841, this painting is
similar to Daubigny's* Saint Jerome *of the
previous year's Salon. Both paintings were a
result of wedding the concept of the "noble
landscape" to direct studies of nature.*

103

Road in the Woods. c. 1844–46
Oil on canvas, 22⅞ × 19 (58 × 48)
Collections: William H. Stuart, 1898;
Collis P. Huntington
Lent by the Metropolitan Museum of Art

*A most charming landscape confessing
Troyon's heritage from the eighteenth century,
but with an almost naïve directness that rivals
Corot.*

104

Landscape near Paris. c. 1849
Oil on millboard, 10½ × 18 (27 × 45.5)
Signed lower right: *C. Troyon*
Collections: Thomas Robinson; H. C. Angell
Lent by the Museum of Fine Arts, Boston

105

Pasture in Normandy. 1852
Oil on panel, 15⅛ × 21⅝ (38.5 × 55)
Signed and dated lower left: *C. Troyon 1852*
Collections: Laurent-Richard; E. Secrétan;
Henry Field
Lent by the Art Institute of Chicago

*In his long campaign of 1852 in Normandy,
Troyon began many of his major paintings
that afterward insured his fame. He had by
now thoroughly absorbed Dutch animal
painting which had so enthralled him during
his year in Holland in 1847. This painting
particularly recalls Potter who also used
similar screens of trees in the middle distance.*

106

The Pointer (Le Chien d'arrêt). 1860
Oil on canvas, 64 × 51½ (163 × 131)
Signed and dated lower left: *C. Troyon 1860*
Collections: A. Dreyfus, 1885; E. Secrétan,
1889; Prosper Crabbe; Durand-Ruel; F. L.
Ames; Mrs. Louis A. Frothingham
Lent by the Museum of Fine Arts, Boston

*Beginning in 1854, Troyon made annual visits
in the Touraine to his friend Loisel, who had a
large kennel of hunting dogs which the artist
frequently painted. That this painting was first
exhibited in Brussels, in 1860, is appropriate,
for it is in the lineage of Lowlands animal
painting, including Snyders and Nicolas
Berchem (in whose* Moor Offering a Parrot to a
Lady, *Wadsworth Atheneum, Hartford, there
is a dog in the identical pose). Troyon remains
the best of all the nineteenth-century animal
painters because he was a superb landscape
artist. In this picture both sky and dog are
seen at a moment of tense expectation.*

107

Le Tréport. c. 1860–62
Oil on panel, 10¾ × 15 (27 × 38)
Signed lower left: *C. Troyon*
Collection: Van Praet, 1893
Lent by the Johnson Collection

*Painted about the time Boudin, on Corot's
advice, was working with Troyon. It shows
that Troyon was capable of significant
contributions to landscape as well as to animal
painting.*

108

Landscape
Red-brown chalk on paper, 20 × 26½
(50.8 × 67.3)
Signed lower right: *C. T.*
Lent by Miss Aimée Lamb, courtesy of
the Fogg Art Museum

102

103

104

105

107

108

BARBIZON

HERITAGE

109

CLAUDE MONET
Le Pavé de Chailly. c. 1867
Oil on canvas, 38¼ × 51⅛ (97.2 × 129.8)
Signed lower right: *Claude Monet*
Lent by Mr. Sam Salz

110

CAMILLE PISSARRO
Peasants Resting. 1881
Oil on canvas, 32 × 25¾ (81 × 65)
Signed lower right: *C. Pissarro 81*
Lent by the Toledo Museum of Art

111

GEORGES PIERRE SEURAT
Farm Women at Work. 1882

Oil on canvas, 15⅛ × 18¼ (38.4 × 46.3)
Lent by the Solomon R. Guggenheim
Museum

112

ALFRED SISLEY
Village Street in Marlotte. 1866
Oil on canvas, 25⅝ × 36 (50 × 92)
Signed lower left: *A. Sisley 1866*
Lent by the Albright-Knox Art Gallery

113

VINCENT VAN GOGH
Peasants Digging. 1889
Oil on canvas, 28¼ × 36¼ (72 × 92)
Lent by Ir. V. W. van Gogh,
on loan Stedelijk Museum

109

111

112

113

This catalogue was set in Monotype Walbaum and Ornata by Clarke & Way, Inc., New York and printed letterpress and bound by them; offset sections are by The Meriden Gravure Co., Meriden, Connecticut; color plates by Joh. Enschedé en Zonen, Haarlem, Holland. Text paper is Mohawk Superfine, by Mohawk Paper Mills, Inc., Cohoes, New York. Color printing on paper furnished by Enschedé. Catalogue designed by Carl F. Zahn, Museum of Fine Arts, Boston.